ISBN 978-1-332-10885-5
PIBN 10285799

1 MONTH OF
FREE
READING

at

www.ForgottenBooks.com

By purchasing this book you are eligible for one month membership to ForgottenBooks.com, giving you unlimited access to our entire collection of over 700,000 titles via our web site and mobile apps.

To claim your free month visit:
www.forgottenbooks.com/free285799

Similar Books Are Available from
www.forgottenbooks.com

Campbell's
Tea, Coffee and
Spice Manual

A Comprehensive Trade Manual

on

Teas, Coffees and Spices

Price $4.80 Net

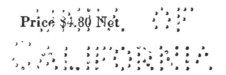

Published by

Lute E. Campbell

316 W. Second St.

Los Angeles, California

Compiled
and
Published by

LUTE E. CAMPBELL

For the information and
protection of Merchants
and
Dedicated to those interested

The writer does not challenge Criticism, but honestly courts it. If, in the perusal of this work, you find an error, or an article, which, in your judgment, is incorrect, or incomplete, and you have more authentic "data" at hand, please forward same to the author.

He will at all times be glad to receive honest criticism, reliable information, opinions and suggestions from those interested in and acquainted with the subjects herein treated.

Any special information cheerfully furnished for the asking, if obtainable.

THE AUTHOR.

C.

429040

AN ALIBI

The writer first turned his attention toward Teas and Coffees in the early eighties, when the public knew scarcely any other than **China** and **Japan Teas,** and at which time, and for many years thereafter, the same unsuspecting public were **buying** principally **Mocha** and **Java Coffee,** and **drinking** principally **Rio,** together with some **Central American** Coffees.

In the course of time he graduated from a wholesale grocery salesman to a Tea and Coffee specialty salesman, thence to a **Tea** and **Coffee** specialist (so-called), thence to a **blender** of **Coffees,** with accumulated experience as a roaster—at the same time a **blender** of **Teas,** with a reasonable degree of success, and finally to a **buyer** and **blender** of both Teas and Coffees for Wholesale Grocers, Tea and Coffee Houses and Wholesale Roasters, and is at this time acting in the capacity of **buyer** and **blender** of **Teas** and **Coffees** for one of the largest and most prominent Wholesale Grocers and Coffee Roasters on the Pacific Coast. While he has never had the temerity to call himself an expert, he has, during these many years, accumulated a considerable fund of knowledge and experience, and knowing from the latter just how hard it is to acquire the former, he has compiled the following for those interested in **Teas, Coffees, Spices, etc.**

The data herein contained is the result of years of study, research and experience, and the writer's thorough personal acquaintance with the **Tea** and **Coffee** shrubs and their cultivation, culture, growth, harvesting, etc., both in the **Gardens** and upon the **plantation.** The condensed papers (prepared in many instances especially for the writer and this work) from Tea, Coffee and Spice Buyers, Brokers and salesmen from China, Japan, Java, Ceylon and India, on Teas, and South and Central America and

Mexico, on Coffees, from clippings from various periodicals, Encyclopedias and various sources of authority, as well as Government reports and Bulletins. and will not only be found to be more than ordinarily authentic and reliable, but should be of incalculable help and value to all desiring information on the subjects treated.

The writer also wishes to refer to **Coffee** papers by such old and prominent writers as Mr. W. P. Hieru, Prof. A. H. Church, Mr. Preston, and Mr. Ellis; to **Tea** papers by Mr. J. L. Shand, of Ceylon; **Hellyer & Co.**, Chicago; J. C. Whitney & Co., New York; **Carter-Macy Co.**, New York; also **P. L. Simmonds' F. L. S., F. R. C. I.**, works published in London on Teas, Coffees, Seeds and Spices; also to Fluckiger & Hanbury's "History of the Principal Drugs"; to Mr. James McPherson's article on **Tea** in the Journal of the Society of Arts, and to Mr. J. Miers' paper on "Maté" in the "Transactions of the Linnean Society, 1861", in "Annals and Magazine of Natural History."

Extracts from the above authorities, segregated and arranged by the author for the **information, convenience and protection of brokers, merchants** and **salesmen.**

Also general information and expressions through and from intimate acquaintance with the **Tea** and **Coffee Trade Journal,** 79 Wall Street, New York, and the **Simmons Spice** Mill, 79 Water Street, New York.

The leading **Tea, Coffee** and **Spice Journals** in the United States and, in the writer's opinion, the **most reliable authority in the world.**

Emphatically **emphasized** points throughout this work are points that should be **especially remembered,** for in most instances they will not only be the particular subject in hand, but will be among the information **most desired.**

AMERICA'S FOREIGN COFFEE TRADING

The foreign Coffee trade of the United States, according to statistics prepared by the Bureau of Foreign and Domestic Commerce, approximated normal, with high record shipments and increased average prices during the fiscal year 1919. Receipts exceeded those of the "peace" year 1914 by only 4.5 per cent and were 8.2 per cent below those of 1918, the last full year of the war. Shipments (that is, exports and re-exports to foreign countries and sales to non-contiguous territories of the United States), on the other hand, were 87.4 per cent greater in quantity and 116.4 per cent greater in value than in 1914, and also surpassed, in both quantity and value, those of 1918.

The average price of the coffee received in 1919 was 13.7 cents a pound, contrasted with 9 cents in 1918, and a shade over 11 cents in 1914; and the average price of the coffee (both domestic and foreign) shipped was 18.6 cents compared with 13 cents in 1918 and 16.1 cents in 1914. As regards domestic raw coffee alone, the average export price was 19.5 cents in 1919, 14.5 cents in 1918, and 16.2 cents in 1914.

The United States has long been the largest Coffee consuming country in the world in the aggregate, though not per capita, but with the advent of nation-wide prohibition, an increase in the per capita consumption is expected, with the once popular "coffee house" of England to supplant the "bar."

COFFEE HISTORY

The early history of Coffee is only to be gleaned from mythology, at least to a great extent. It is claimed by many to have been native to Abyssinia and Ethiopia; however, the concensus of opinion seems to be that the civilized world is indebted to Africa for the Coffee Bean.

Its early history is clouded in tradition, but it appears to have been known by the **Ethiopians** of **Northern Africa** from time immemorial. It was not, however, used in the form of a **beverage**, but was toasted, or roasted, crushed and mixed with **animal fats** and rolled into **balls** about the size of a billiard ball. These were used **as food**: one of them, it is said, being capable of sustaining a man for a day. It was preferred by these people to either meat or bread, as it cheered as well as sustained. Its use reached **Abyssinia** toward the end of the thirteenth century, and traveled about two hundred years later into Arabia. It is claimed that **Coffee** was first introduced into **Arabia** in the year 875 A. D., but it did not come into popular favor until the discovery of its excellence as a **beverage** in the first part of the fifteenth century.

This discovery from the mythological accounts we have of it, was purely accidental. It is said that a certain ruler of some **Dervishes** had a flock of goats, and that he had noticed their antics after **feasting** on the **berries** from the **Coffee** tree. Now, this **ruler** had been greatly annoyed by the tendency of his **Dervishes** to "sleep in church", even at this early date, and he was led to believe that if he could in some way induce them to eat a few beans off this aformentioned bush, that they would stay awake during service, be interested and happy. How was he to get them to partake of this little berry? Ah! an **infusion** of it would shroud its origin in the necessary cloak of mystery. It worked like a charm and was soon the hit of the hour, to such an extent, in fact, that it fell under the ban of the church, and was expressly forbidden in the **Koran**, but without avail—**Coffee** had come to stay.

The **Arabs**, however, guarded their secret jealously, and it was almost a hundred years before it was introduced into Turkey. **Arabia** seems to have been the stepping-stone for the universal consumption of **Coffee**, and it was **Arabian Coffee** shipped through the port of Mocha that shed a halo around the name "Mocha" and led the Coffee world into using it as a panoply for millions of tons that never saw Arabia. In those days Arabian merchants were considered the most enterprising in the world. They stood at the gateway from Asia to Europe, and they added the Coffee bean from Africa to the spices and other luxuries of the Orient.

The use of Coffee quickly spread outward: first to Persia and Syria, then to Cairo, and in a few years to Venice.

Then an Arab and an Abyssinian, by names Shem and Heken, opened the first Coffee house in Constantinople, and introduced the Turkish public to this new delight. It took like wildfire, and their house was thronged day and night, and Oriental Coffee houses sprang up everywhere in the city. It is said that the poorer classes even begged money in the streets to purchase Coffee. It was soon a firm habit with the Turkish people, and we are told that at one time there was an edict issued to the effect that "failure" to supply a wife with a specified amount of Coffee per diem, was admitted to be a valid cause for divorce. As in Arabia, the drinking of Coffee was opposed on religious grounds, but with the same results.

It was not until 1615 that Coffee was allowed to tickle the Western palate. This was brought over by some Venetian merchants, and served to their friends, but at this time the price was prohibitive, and it was not until 1650 that it was publicly introduced in Europe. At this time a London merchant brought over a quantity of Arabian Coffee and an Armenian servant to prepare it. He intended serving it to his friends and customers. It proved an instantaneous success with the English public. He found his place so thronged with Coffee drinkers, that he was unable to conduct his business. Thereupon he gave his Armenian a tent placed on a side street, and

11

here was opened the first **English Coffee House**, followed by others rapidly. These were tremendously popular and became the gathering places of the famous **wits** and **nobility** of the day, and developed into our **modern club**.

The progress of the **Coffee** bean was beset with many obstacles. Although **Coffee** was immediately popular, it had no easy road in **England**. It was opposed from every point of view—**medical, moral,** physical and **political,** and was excessively **taxed**. Religiously inclined people denounced **Coffee** as an insidiously pernicious beverage. **Statesmen** saw political danger in the discussions which marked the attendance at the **Coffee** houses. On this ground they were **closed** by **Government** orders on several occasions, and in several countries; and governments found new sources of revenue by heavy **taxation** on every gallon of **Coffee** brewed, but the beverage proved its real popularity and worth by out-living all restrictions.

In 1671 the first **Coffee house** or **cafe** was opened in **Marseilles**. It proved immediately popular, and the **cafes** soon rivalled the older cabarets in attendance. It was, however, not popular at this time with the **Nobility**. **Louis XIV** did not like **Coffee**, consequently his **Court** did not. It became popular with the **Nobility** immediately, however, upon his death, and it is said that the family of **Louis XV** spent $12,000 to $15,000 a year to have **Coffee** on their table.

For about fifty years after the advent of **Coffee** in **Europe**, the entire supply came from **Arabia**—**Mocha Coffee**, so called from the port from which it was shipped. About 1690, however, the **Dutch** appeared in the Worlds Market with large quantities of **Java**, and from this time on the growing of **Coffee** soon spread into all parts of the **Tropical** world.

It was introduced into **India** in about 1700, and about twenty years later into **Ceylon** from **Java** by the **Dutch,** and in 1740 into the **Phillipines** by **Spanish** Missionaries from **Java,** and at about this time the first shrub or tree was planted in **Brazil,** now the world's greatest Coffee growing country, and a little later it spread to **Cuba, Porto Rico** and **Mexico,** and then to practically all parts of **South** and **Central America.** Today Africa, the original source is a comparatively unimportant factor in the production of **Coffee,** how ever, considerable is marketed from the **Liberian** districts.

In every instance, in all countries, the public's instantaneous acceptance of this delightful beverage, although it has been opposed from every point of view, shows that a commodity for which there is a universal craving among mankind, civilized or savage, cannot be denied, regardless of the opposition it incurs, and it is today the sole hot beverage of more than a hundred million people.

FROM THE SEED TO THE CUP

The **Coffee** bean of commerce is the seed of a fruit, resembling in size and shape a large cranberry very much. However, its general appearance is more frequently referred to as like a medium sized cherry, and is yellowish-red to purple-red when ripe.

The fruit of the "Cherry" so called, is made up thus: Beginning from the outside: An outside skin resembling the skin of a cherry in texture— A soft pulp—Then a soft glutinous substance, containing a quantity of saccharine, then a parchment coating resembling the husk of wheat; then the "Silver-Skin" (like the onion skin). Within this are usually two Coffee beans; when only one bean is found inside the "Cherry" or "Berry" (This occurs occasionally in all varieties and frequently in a few) the "flat side" (?) still holds the distinguishing groove, but it is nearly as round as the other. These beans are known as "pea-berries", "male-berries" or "Caracolillo" (Mexican) or "Caracole". They are most plentiful on old bushes or trees.

The Coffee "berry" is the fruit of an evergreen tree, which in its natural growth is rather slender and attains a height of from five to thirty feet. The plant of commerce, however, is dwarfed to about five feet. This seems to render it more sturdy, and also convenient for gathering.

There are many varieties of Coffee plants, but all having the same general characteristics. Botanists seem to differ as to whether or not they are really divisible into different families. Popularly speaking, there are two general types. The Arabian, which is the old type, furnishes practically all of the Coffee of commerce, even the Brazillian and Java Coffee belongs to this type. The Liberian is a comparatively new type and was discovered in the wilds of Liberia, (Western Africa). It is now cultivated extensively in several countries including Brazil, the Dutch East Indies, Ceylon and Java, the latter name sometimes being coupled with it and called African Java or Liberian Java.

The Maragogipi, a native of Brazil, together with Liberian Coffees are receiving considerable attention on account of the more hardy growth of the plants and the larger size of the bean. They have not the fine cup quality of the Arabian Coffee, but their size and strength enhance their value for blending.

Robusta Coffee is a late arrival in the Coffee world, and has been received by many with considerable favor. It is a very mild characterless Coffee and practically neutral used with other Coffees; is usually to be had at a low price and is frequently used as a "filler" in both the cheap and medium priced blends.

The Coffee plant requires a warm climate and very warm nights. The soil must be deep and well drained, and there must be rain every month, and from one hundred to one hundred and fifty inches within the year.

The **Arabian** variety grows best at an elevation of from 2500 to 5000 feet, and the **Liberian** grows well at 1500 feet down to almost **sea level.**

The plant is grown from seed and generally begins to bear after **three** to **five** years. The leaves are oblong, dark glossy-green on the upper surface, and rather a pale-green underneath, from five to six inches long, and two or three inches in width. The flowers are white and fragrant, slightly resembling the Jesamine in odor and grow in great clusters in the axils of the leaves. The fruit quickly follows the flower; the flesh or pulp of the fruit is sweet and agreeable in flavor, and is frequently eaten by the pickers. The berries must be **taken** (picked) from the trees when ripe, as otherwise they fall from the tree and are lost to the planter.

There are generally **two** or **three main harvests** in the course of a year, and cultivation aims to direct the crops as closely to that end as possible, but to a greater or less degree, the plant bears blossoms and fruit the year round.

The Coffee beans are at first of a soft bluish or greenish color, becoming hard and flinty on exposure, and changing usually with age to a pale yellowish tint and occasionally almost a golden hue.

There are two methods of gathering these berries. In the old, or **Arabian method, cloths** are **spread** on the ground and the ripe berries are allowed to fall into **these.** This insures getting full ripe berries, and raises the standard of the crop decidedly, due to the **ripeness** of the berry.

The other method which is in use in practically all of the world, consists in **gathering** the berry **by hand.** This method is used in practically every coffee raising country at the present time, with the exception of **Arabia,** and has the disadvantage that some **green** (immature) berries are gathered which often materially lowers the standard of the crop. This may be guarded against, however, by plunging the berries, at any time until roasted, into a bath of water. The **green berries** are light and will float, and these should be thrown away.

The **next** process consists of removing the skin and pulp. By the old, or "sun-dried" method, still in use in some countries, the berries are placed in the sun to dry. Then when fully dry, the skin and pulp are removed by pounding in wooden mortars and winnowed. This method has the disadvantage that some of the berries are crushed or broken, thereby lowering the quality of the batch, but, being dried in the sun in the original skin, all of the flavor is retained, and for this reason it is said to produce more desired results from the consumers point of view, though the quality is lower from a marketing view point.

In the **other** method, called the **West Indian process,** the berries are pulped the same day they are gathered, being run between two rollers. Next, water is let in and the pulp floated away, being saved for use as a fertilizer, or as a Coffee substitute. The "parchment" beans are then put into a cistern for the removal of the glutinous coating. This is removed by one of two methods. In the popular method water is added to the berries in the cistern, and they are allowed to set about forty-eight hours. The water is then run off and the berries are washed free of the coating. The other method consists of putting the berries into the cistern without water and allowing them to **ferment,** the coating then removed as in the former method. The latter method is preferable from the consumers view point, since it is claimed that in allowing the berries to set in the water for two days, some of the flavor and aroma is lost.

16

The berries are dried, preferably in the sun, when the air is not too damp and hot, but if there is danger of fermentation, which will take place under these conditions, they are machine dried. This method does not seem to have any injurious effect on the quality of the Coffee produced.

The berries are then run through a "peeler," and the parchment and "silver-skin" removed, the waste being winnowed away. They are then sorted according to size, cleaned of rubbish, trash, etc., and packed.

The method of sizing or grading varies: sometimes an inclined revolving cylindrical sieve, divided into different sized meshes is used; again in some of the more up-to-date plantations, separators of the eccentric or vibrator type have succeeded the former method. The separation in either method is followed up by a careful sorting over by hand, especially of the better grades.

In olden times the product was now ready for market, as practically everyone roasted their own Coffee; now-a-days, however, by far the greater part of the Coffee sold is already roasted.

This roasting, although it is not generally known by the people, is a very precarious propositiou, because the best Coffee poorly roasted, is poor Coffee. If over roasted, the "snap" and fragrance is gone—if under done, it tastes grassy, green and raw, and makes a very poor cup. Ten seconds either way might spoil the roast.

The roasting is done in large revolving drums or cylinders, under which a brisk fire is kept and regulated according to the type of Coffee being roasted. The Coffee must be constantly turned to roast regularly, and should be roasted quite rapidly in order to protect and retain the active principles. When properly roasted, it should be cooled as quickly as possible to prevent loss of strength, and then should be immediately packed in closely sealed containers, preferably air tight, as the oil cells have been broken open by the heat action and the volatile oil containing the aroma of the Coffee is quickly dissipated.

Generally Coffee aged two or three years makes the best roast from the point of drinking qualities.

According to good authority (and the writer's opinion) the Coffee is just now ready for blending, however, it is a later day custom to blend the green Coffees and then roast. This custom is followed very extensively, but there is no question but the different sized beans and the different aged berries, and the green and dry berries require different treatment in the roaster.

In blending, we know that some Coffees have Aroma, some have Flavor, and some Strength, Body, Character. The unknown quantity in blending is the "public palate." We have to consider only what they will like. After we have determined on the favored blend, we should adhere strictly to it—this is quite a task and requires good taste and discernment, for it must be borne in mind that the essential qualities of the Coffee berry varies—this year's crop is not exactly like last year's crop from the same tree— nor is the berry in a given district identical with the same berry in another part of the same district, so it may readily be seen that great care must be taken to maintain the standard of any special blend, and can only be accomplished by painstakingly cupping and tasting the liquors from various types until "matched."

The Coffee classifications best known to the general public are "Mocha," "Java," "Maracaibo," "Colombian," "Santos," "Bourbon Santos," "Liberian," "Rio," "Guatemala" and "Pea-Berry" (or Caracole).

The cheapest varieties of general consumption are low grade Rio's, and the dearest the high grade Mochas and Javas or East Indian.

18

So much for the cultivation and preparation of Coffee. Let us now consider how it is judged for marketing.

COFFEE SELECTION

Vast experience is essential to the training of a Coffee Expert.

The chapters following on the different Coffee growths give brief descriptions of the beans of the principal varieties, but there are so many different kinds, so much alike and yet so many minor differences of size, appearance, color and cup quality, that very few people can correctly judge the quality of a bean by its appearance raw, and only the keenest experts can determine its classification after roasting.

Coffees are judged first by the form of the bean. There being three general types in this regard, but in as much as some Coffee plants bear beans of all three types, this is but a summary test.

The best test for a layman is by a sample infusion after roasting and grinding.

The next test is the size. The medium sized bean of any variety, is generally regarded as possessing the finest flavor, but there is no fixed standard as to size, as this varies with the localities, where the beans are cultivated, the kind of season—whether wet or dry, and various other reasons.

Color is the next test—in which we find a variation all the way from a transparent yellow to a bluish-green, dark-brown or black.

Each geographical division has a different standard of color, and also every locality of distribution has different requirements. For example: in buying "**Rio**" we note that Chicago wants medium to light green. Cincinnati, yellow. Louisville, yellow and dark-green. Texas, darkest-green. And each market is willing to pay a premium to get the shade it wants.

The **place of production** is the next requirement. This is based mainly on what those names mean to the public. Mocha being the first Coffee used, was immortalized in song and story, so naturally the largest demand is for **Mocha**, consequently if it looks like **Mocha**, it's in demand.

The next requirement is the geographical location of the place of production—whether **highland** or **lowland**. The highlands produce much better grades of Coffee, as it is firmer textured, not so watery or grassy of flavor.

The next considerations are the **smell, flavor, uniformity, age** and absence of foreign particles. While on the subject of age, it may be of interest to note that Coffee takes an **added quality with age,** like wine, and it is said that artificial ageing is done just prior to the roasting. It is determined by the color of the bean, which must be well washed to determine "premature age."

The final **step** in judging Coffee is the roasting, when the Aroma, etc., is observed. The Coffee is then ground and an infusion made for the purpose of **observing** the **flavor, body, etc.**

As to the range in quality—it is too wide to be discussed here. For example, Brazilian Coffee is first divided into ten grades, ranging in quality from the equal of the best **Mocha** down to the poorest Mexican, and in truth the most of the Mocha (?), until recently, was "Golden Rio." Then the quality varies again every year, as to the size and quality of the crop produced and the general condition of the market.

An analysis of Coffee follows:

Moisture 11.22
Oils and Fats 14.27
Albumen 6.96
Caffeine 1.18
Ash 3.51
Caffeo ⎫
Matter soluble in water ⎬........24.87
Tannic acid, etc. ⎭

Of these ingredients, Caffeo, the esential oil, Caffeine alkaloid, the stimulant and Tannic Acid, the astringent, concern us most. Let us consider them separately.

Caffeine gives to Coffee its delicious aroma when roasting. It produces a slight, gentle perspiration, an agreeable excitement. and stimulates the mental faculties. It retards in a marked degree the waste of tissue, and has a slight aperient effect on the bowels.

Caffeine has no odor and a bitter taste. It increases nervous activity, enlivens the imagination and increases the heart and pulse.

Tannic Acid is an astringent. To it is ascribed the flavor and chief properties of Coffee as a beverage.

When we consider these together in combination, we have a combination that exhilirates, arouses and keeps awake, counteracts the stupor of fatigue, disease and opium. It allays hunger to a certain extent and gives the weary increased strength and vigor.

Physiologically, it makes the brain more active, yet soothes the body, and lessens the change of the tissue, and consequently there is a lesser demand for food.

Taken in moderate quantities, Coffee quickens the gastric juices and relieves the feeling of plentitude after a meal.

The Coffee we get is 73% Brazilian. The rest is mostly Central American, yet the majority of brands of roasted Coffee on the American market, probably 60% of it, until recently, was Mocha and Java Blend. Can you figure it?

Some statistics:

A man picks 120 lbs. of Coffee berries a day.
120 lbs. of berries yield 15 lbs. of dried green beans.
One tree yields 1 to 8 lbs. of Coffee a year.
Coffee loses 5 to 8% in ageing.
Coffee loses 16 to 22% in roasting.

Good Coffee depends upon:

Quality of the seed bean.
Locality where raised—high or low.
Annual amount of rainfall.
Method of picking.
Method of preparing, sun cured or not, dry or wet ferment.
Age, before roasting.
Proper roasting.
Absence of "blights" or "Quakers."
Proper blending.
Proper grinding.
The public palate.

Everyone used to roast his own Coffee.

Coffee loses its aroma and flavor very soon after roasting, and should have every protection possible.

The final process is the grinding, and this should always be done. when possible, immediately before use, as Coffee loses much of its flavor and aroma in a very short while after grinding. This process is much more important than most people realize, and the finished product may be spoiled for a lover of good Coffee by improper grinding. If it is ground too coarsely, you do not get the flavor and strength in the infusion. If it is ground too finely, you get the same effect as in over-boiling, too much Tannic Acid extracted and a biter acrid cup.

Coffee should be differently ground for every method of preparation: e. g., perculator Coffee requires a fine grinding; boiled Coffee a coarse grinding.

Simple tests for ground Coffee are: (1) Press a little of the ground Coffee between the fingers —if it cakes, it is adulterated, probably with Chickory. (2) Place a little of the dry Coffee in a glass of water. If nearly all floats and the water does not color, or only a very little, the Coffee is probably pure. If part sinks, it is adulterated, probably with cereal, chickory or similar substances. If the water turns a deep reddish tint, chickory has been added to it. (3) Spread a little dry Coffee on a piece of glass or something similar and moisten with a few drops of water. Then pick out some of the smallest pieces with a needle, if they are soft, the Coffee is certainly adulterated, as real Coffee bean particles stay hard even after long immersion in water.

It must be remembered that the above tests apply only to the purity of the bean. They tell nothing of the flavor or aroma, which are determining points of value.

A Coffee may be perfectly pure, yet be harsh, musty, hidey or in many ways undesirable, hence the necessity of testing flavor and aroma by making infusion.

In purchasing the raw beans, one should also thoroughly bear in mind that: (1) If all of one variety (i. e., before blending) they should be fairly uniform in size, apeparance and color. (2) They should be free from stems, stones, dirt and all such foreign matter. (3) When cut, they should be the same general color all the way through. If the inside is considerably lighter than the outside, it will usually be found that the beans have been artificially colored. Of recent years, however, this deception has been practiced very little, if any.

THE PRINCIPAL COFFEE GROWING COUNTRIES

Giving the Principal Trade Names, also Districts, Plantations and Chief Characteristics of the Various Coffees.

NORTH AMERICA

Mexico

Colima.
Corodoba.
Chiapas.
Triunfo.
Tabasco.
Tampico.
Tapachula.
Oaxaca. (Pronounced Wahaka or War-har-kar.)
Sierra.
Coatzacoalcos.
Uruapan.
Coatepec. (Tepic)

Central America

Guatemala:—Coban.
Costa Rica.
Salvador: { Santa Anna.
{ Santa Tecia.
Honduras.
Nicaragua.
Belize.

SOUTH AMERICA

Venezuela

Angostura.

La Guaira: { Caracas:—
{ Trillade.
{ Porto Ca-
{   bello.
{ Coro.

Maracaibo: { Cucuta.
{ Merida.
{ Tovar.
{ Salazar.
{ Trujillo.
{ Bocono.
{ Tacharia.

Carupano.

Ecuador

Guayaquil.

Colombia-Sabanilla

Bogota.
Canca.
Jerico.
Bucaramanga.
Antioquia:—Mendellín.
Ocana.
Santa Marta.

Brazil

Rio.
Santos: { Campinas.
{ Bourbon.
Victoria. Capatania.
Ceara. Cuaruaru.

Bahia: { Caravella.
{ Nazareth.
{ Chapada.
{ Minas-Garaes.
{ Maragogipe.

WEST INDIA ISLANDS

Guadeloupe.
Martinique.
Cuba.
Jamaica—Blue Mountain.

Puerto Rico.
Hayti.
San Domingo.
Guracao.

PACIFIC ISLANDS

Hawaiian Islands.
Phillipine Islands.—Ma-
nilla.

ASIA

Arabia

Mocha: $\left\{\begin{array}{l} \text{Yemen} \\ \text{Tehama} \\ \text{Serki} \\ \text{Sanani} \\ \text{Hodeida} \end{array}\right\}$ Short Bean.

Abyssinian

Harrar. (Long bean).
Magrache.

AFRICA

Guinea.
Enconge.
Liberia.
Malabar
Abyssinia.

INDIA

Mysore.

EAST INDIA ISLANDS

Timor.
Bali.
Celebes—Macassar.
Tagal.
Kroe.
Lahat.
Corinche.
Beongie.
Singapore.
Ceylon.
Straits Liberian.
Bonthyne.

Sumatra

Padang: $\left\{\begin{array}{l} \text{Mandheling.} \\ \text{Ankola.} \\ \text{Ayerbangies.} \\ \text{Painan.} \\ \text{Interior.} \\ \text{Indrapoers.} \\ \text{Palembang.} \end{array}\right.$

Private Estate: $\left\{\begin{array}{l} \text{Bockit Gom-} \\ \quad \text{pong.} \\ \text{Soemanik.} \\ \text{Gadoeng Batoe.} \\ \text{Soerian.} \\ \text{Loboe Raya.} \\ \text{Loboe Sampir.} \\ \text{Si Barasap.} \\ \text{Akar Gedand} \\ \text{Merapi.} \\ \text{Taloeg Gedang.} \\ \text{Loeboeg Ge-} \\ \quad \text{dand.} \\ \text{Like.} \\ \text{Soengu Landei.} \\ \text{Soengu Ram-} \\ \quad \text{boekan.} \end{array}\right.$

Java

Bantam.
Batavia.
Buitenzorg.
Preanger.
Krawang.
Cheribon.
Togal.
Banjoemas.
Pekalongan.
Baquilan.
Kadoe.
Samarang.
Pamanoekin. (Liberian.)

Japara.
Soerkarta.
Djokjarkarta.
Madroen.
Remang.
Sourabaya.
Kedire.
Malang.
Pasoeroean.
Probolingo.
Bejreki.
Banjoewangi.

COFFEE CHART

Of the Popular and Commonly Used Types

BRAZIL, SOUTH AMERICA.	Rio	Golden and the numbers
	Santos	Flat Bean / Curley Bean / Red Bean / Bourbon
COLOMBIA, SOUTH AMERICA.	Bucaramanga, Sabanillas Antioquia	
	Bogota's { Medellin / Manizales / Fantassia }	{ Excelso and Extra
CENTRAL AMERICA.	Guatemala	Coban / Costa Cuca / Costa Granda / Costa De Cusha / Tumbador
	Costa Rica	Caracole and the numbers 1st, 2nd, 3rd
	Salvador	Yellow Bean / Green Bean
	Nicaragua	Natural / Washed
	Honduras	Yellow / Heavy / Bean
DUTCH AND BRITISH WEST INDIES	Jamaica (Blue Mountain) / San Domingo / Porto Rican / Haitian / Guantanamo / Alquizar / Marcos / Sierra Maestra	Best Cuban Districts and Plantations
VENEZUELA, SOUTH AMERICA.	Maracaibo	Cucuta / Meridia / Bocona / Tovar / Trujillo
	La Guaira	Caracas / Porto / Cabello / Coro
MEXICAN	Coatepec / Cordoba / Caracolillo / Cordoba	(Tepic) / (Pea Berry) / (Mexican Jack)

26

EAST INDIA, JAVA ISLANDS.	Javas	Plantation Government Blue-Bean or Washed East Indian
EAST INDIA SUMATRA ISLANDS.	Mandheling Ankola	Javas
EAST INDIA, JAVA ISLANDS.	Liberian Robusta	Java Coffee Laurentii
ARABIA	Mocha	Yemen Grades Tehama Nos. 1, 1A, Sanani 2, 3
	Harrar (Longberry) Abyssianian	
CEYLON	"Native" "Plantation" Liberian- Ceylon (Liberian Hybrid) Ceylon (Arabia Seed)	
INDIA	Malabar Mysore	
ECUADOR	Guayaquils	
HAWAIIAN	Konos	
PHILLIPPINES	Luzon Manila Zamboanjo	

All Coffee plants produce some Caracole (Pea berry).

Some types are always "unwashed." However, most types may be had "washed" or natural.

DIVISIONS

The first division of Coffee is into "strong" and "mild." The Rio's and some of the Santos are commonly said to constitute the "strong" varieties. (However, the writer considers it correct to include Liberians and some of the hybrids). The other part of the Santos crop and practically all the importations of the other kinds, come under the heading of milds.

The next classification by the Wholesale Merchant is by the Country of Export, sub-divided in each case into various growths and grades.

The best known Brazil **Coffees** are the **Rios** and **Santos.**

Rio Coffees are heavy in body and with a distinctive flavor and aroma, in fact in most instances **Rio Coffees** are strong to rankness but properly built around in blends, help to produce a very fine strong drink. Individually they are generally of a very pungent character. Again, however, some of the Higher Types, such as, say, "Golden Rio" are of fine character and are splendid in the cup. The beans vary in size and color from large to small, and dark green to light yellow. But in the main, **Rio Coffee** is a low grade Brazilian growth of a very pronounced, **strong,** even **rank flavor,** and is rapidly losing favor in the eyes of the best informed trade.

It is now only used in limited sections of the United States to any extent. It has been remarked that one bag of **Rio** mixed with ten bags of any other **Coffee** would produce **eleven** bags of —**Rio.** Formerly it was thought that **Rio** combined with **Java** produced a satisfactory blend.

SANTOS COFFEES

Santos Coffees are generally milder than "Rios" and very smooth and pleasing in the cup, not so full as many types, but very mellow and a splendid blender with most types, excepting, perhaps, **East Indian** or **Javas,** e. g., such as **Padangs, Macassars, Mandhelings,** etc. Some authority has said it is like mixing cream with water to try to blend **Santos** with the latter named **Coffees,**—"it would be better to buy milk to begin with"; at any rate the writer has never been successful in blending the two types.

The finer grades of **Santos** are of such excellent quality that they have been widely substituted for even high grade **Javas** and **Mochas** (practiced but little if any now), the "curley bean" being used in the latter case. They range from large to small, and from green and rich yellow to very pale yellow.

For purposes of exchange transactions, it is customary to term any Coffee shipped through the port of Santos, Santos Coffee.

The City of Santos is the shipping center of the State of Sao Paulo, Brazil, and is the World's greatest Coffee port.

"Red Bean Santos" is obtained from the Campinas district. It is considered more "flavory" and richer than the yellow or greenish varieties.

"Bourbon Santos" is a small bean variety (sometimes called "curley bean") which has grown rapidly in popularity on account of its winey or vinous character. It was formerly sold as "Mocha" or "Mocha Seed" and is even now sometimes spoken of as the "Mocha" of South America. It was originally grown from Mocha seed (Coffee Arabica). The bean for the first two or three crops looks like a Mocha bean and makes a handsome roast. In appearance it should be small, partially round crinkley bean, and, if a genuine Bourbon Santos, should more nearly resemble "Mocha Coffee" with reference to style and cup character than any other Coffee.

"Flat Bean Santos." After the third year of bearing, the Bourbon or Mocha Seed Santos takes on a flat bean characteristic which causes it to be spoken of thereafter as Flat Bean Santos.

The State of Sao Paulo, Brazil, produces the Santos Coffee, so called because it is shipped through the port of Santos. Santos Coffee harvest takes place in May and June, and the average crop of beans obtained from each tree varies from one to six pounds. (In some cases more possibly).

The principal types cultivated in Sao Paulo are: The Bourbon, Creoulo, Amarelio and Maragogipe.

The **Borbon** is the most delicate and **short** lived tree, but the **greatest producer,** usually producing an abundant crop, but the beans are the smallest of the four principal varieties.

The other three do not produce so abundantly, but are long-lived and hardy. The **Creoulo.** or common **native** variety, and the **Amarelio** or yellow variety bear **yellow** instead of **red** berries, (or Cherries) and the **Maragogipe** grows on the largest **tree,** has the largest beans. (So large in fact, as to be called freakish, frequently). The **Coffees** produced by these varieties are classified on the estates according to size, shape and pureness of quality, into: **Fine Moka, Fine Flat, Superior, Good, Regular, Ordinary** and **Refuse.** These are classified in **types** ranging from **one to nine** inclusive—One, Two and Three being the best. Type one does not have a single black bean. **Six** black beans per pound are permissible in Type Two. Type Three is allowed **thirteen black** beans to the pound. The two first Types are not to be found on the market. The scarcity of Type Three makes Type Four the commercial **base** for these Coffees. This Type is allowed to contain up to thirty black beans to the pound. To designate the quality, **black** beans increase in number until Type **Nine** is allowed **850** in a single pound and lower, the classification proportionately. Type **Seven** poor quality with 200 black beans per pound is usually about 13 or 14 cents per Ten Pounds Cheaper than Type **Four.** (Black beans are commonly called "Quakers.")

In addition to the foregoing, the State of Sao Paulo grows some of all different types and qualities of Coffee known in all parts of the world.

The winey or vinous character of the **Bourbon Santos** is frequently alluded to as **acid** or **acidy.** In the estimation of the writer such terms as **acid, acidy** or **non-acidy** applied to Coffee not only maligns a wholesome product, but is positively erroneous. In all the accumulated "data" covering a period of thirty years, I have never read a chemical analysis showing a Bourbon (or flat bean) to contain either more or less acid than any other Coffee. It is true that some Coffees have a more distinct, "stand-outish" or winey flavor than others, the same as some Coffees are stronger than others—in either case the distinctiveness is brought about no doubt. first, from the origin of the seed and then from soil, altitude or climatic conditions or the combination of these conditions.

Among the numerous other types of Brazilian Coffee are "Victoria" or Capotuica, Bahia and Liberian Rio.

The most generally accepted grades of "Rio" and "Santos" are from 1 to 10, or as follows

Fancy:—Large and uniform in color and in size: clear and perfect in selection and attractive in general appearance, divided into "light," "medium" and "dark."

Prime:—Very clear and regular in color and size, but not so rich in appearancee as "Fancy."

Good:—Uniform in color and size, but ranging from "Clear" to "Strictly Clear." Divided into "Light," "Medium" and "Dark." This is the average or standard grade, now quoted as 4s commercially.

Fair:—Only moderate and liable to contain many black (commonly called "Quakers") broken and otherwise imperfect beans.

Ordinary:—Irregular in color and size and liable to contain many black broken beans and a proportion of hulls, etc.

Common:—The lowest grade, mixed with bad and broken beans, chaff, hulls, etc.

COLOMBIA, BUCARAMANGA, BOGATA, "SABANILLA"

Colombia:—A State located in the extreme northern part of South America, also lightly touching the west coast.

Colombia is and has been for years one of our most important producers of fine Coffees, and its natural advantages promise still more abundant production.

Being near the Equator, Colombian Coffees may be raised at a much higher altitude than is possiple in most countries.

Quality in Coffee depends upon high altitudes more than any other single condition, hence the High Grade.

BOGOTAS AND BUCARAMANGAS

The City of Bogota is approximately 9000 feet above the sea level. Bucaramanga is slightly lower. The districts surrounding produce among the choicest grades of Coffee in the world. These Coffees (particularly the Bucaramanga). when extra well aged, as was the case during the Venezuelan war, take on such a rich brown color and show such mellowness in the cup as to be indistinguishable when placed beside Mandhelings and Ankolas of Sumatra, either in appearance or the cup.

The Bogotas properly speaking are produced in a district of small area; in fact the production of the true Bogota is limited to perhaps 12,000 to 18,000 bags a year, however, the Coffees raised in the districts of Manizales, Antioquia, Honda and Canca are generally bought and sold as Bogotas, and with the exception of the last named, these districts produce some excellent Coffees, particularly the fancy grades.

Good grade Bogotas possess splendid winey body, and flavor, and when aged make wonderful individual drinkers.

Bogotas of particularly "winey" character are good to use with (or in place of) Mocha and Harrar for cost reduction and improving the appearance for Abyssinian Coffee usually carries many "quakers" and Arabian is generally insignificant to look upon.

The Bucaramanga and Bogotas, which are the two best known varieties of Colombia, rank among the finest of American Coffees.

Bucaramanga and the district by that name is a good ten days or two weeks journey from Bogota with mules.

The finest Bucaramangas are the Naturals (unwashed), particularly when the season and climate gives them a well browned growth. It is then that these Coffees have such heavy bo_{dy} as to be called the "backbone" of blends. Fine Javas and Sumatras are but slightly superior; in fact, Bucaramangas of this type, and particularly well aged, will do practically the same work of Javas: they are possibly not quite so winey or flavory, but their extraordinary strength makes 10 to 20 per cent a strong factor in "blends."

Good grade Colombian Coffees produce 25% more strength in the cup than the same weight in Santos, and gives a flavor and aroma unobtainable from Santos.

Bucaramangas are frequently referred to as "Bucs."

Savanillas are sometimes sold as "Bucs" but never carry the heavy body for which the Bucaramangas are used. So called Savanillas are usually Maracaibos. Some Colombians, however, are correctly known as "Savanillas" commercially. A good Maracaibo is more desirable than the cheaper "Bucs."

The **Bucaramanga** bean is large and solid, and the liquor full **bodied, fragrant** and **aromatic;** when **aged** it develops a very rich dark brown color. This is a good individual drinker, and as a **blender** follows **Mochas, Harrars** and **Javas** very closely, and is frequently used (when well aged) very successfully in blends as a substitute for **Java.**

Bogota is a mountain grown Coffee, the bean large, uniform and bluish-green, and the liquor full-bodied, round and fragrant. It is the **basis** of a great number of high-grade blends. They roast evenly and have a handsome color. When green many of them are rather rough in appearance, but with all a very high individual type.

Medellin and **Manizales** are, in the best grades, also very highly considered.

Other lesser types are **Canca, Ocana,** etc. **Ocana** is a town situated in a province of the same name in **Colombia, South America.** Coffee from this province was, and still is, to a limited extent, classed as **Maracaibo** Coffee, but is decidedly inferior in appearance, roast and drink, and is used principally as a filler.

Manizales Coffees are so called from the town of that name, located in **Colombia, South America,** near **Medellin,** from which certain varieties of **Colombian** or **Bogota** Coffees are shipped.

Fantassia Coffee is "**Excelso**" and "**Extra**" combined, or before they are separated or graded.

Excelso is a fancy Coffee from any **Colombian** Coffee district, and is composed of the large handsome beans.

Extra is the smaller beans. In other words, **Fantassia** separated produces the two last named types.

Medellin, Capital City of Antioquia, Colombia, South America, and a name given to the **finest** growths of **Colombian** Coffees. This Coffee comes from the mountainous regions, and is given the preference over all other Colombian Coffees, with the possible exception of the Old Bucaramangas.

Antioquia. Name applied to a high grade Coffee grown in Colombia, South America. What is known in the United States as "Medellin" is in reality Antioquia Coffee, and is very typey.

VENEZUELA: MARACAIBO, LA GUAIRA

The two best types of Venezuela Coffee are Maracaibo and La Guaira.

Maracaibos are divided into several varieties, among them Cucuta, Merida, Bocono, Tovar and Trujillo (the lowest) graded as washed (the best) prime to choice, fair to good, ordinary, etc.

Both the Cucuta and the Merida in good season, often equal the finest Coffees grown anywhere. The beans are large, round and solid, rich yellow in appearance and make a fine rich liquor of full ripe flavor.

The Maracaibo district is in Venezuela, South America, and is situated on a Bay of Lake Maracaibo. It is from this district that the bulk of Venezuelean Coffees are shipped.

The Maracaibo type comes from the mountain slopes of Merida, Trujillo and Tachira.

Merida. Coffee named from a town in Venezuela, located near Lake Maracaibo. This is the finest growth of Venezuelean (Maracaibo) Coffee. This Coffee makes a good roast and has a peculiarly delicate flavor; neither winey or bitter, and is much prized by experts.

Bocono, Tovar and Trujillo Coffees are generally smaller and less attractive in appearance, and their liquor is light, but they are useful for blending, as their flavor is usually pleasant. These Coffees blend well with Bourbon Santos.

La Guaira Coffees are best known by the Caracas, Porto Cabello and Coro types. Choice "washed" **Caracas** is exceptionally fine Coffee; **rich, heavy and fragrant;** the bean is **large and bluish.** Caracas is the Capital of **Venezuela.**

"Mild" **Caracas** makes only a fair liquor. The bean is yellowish and medium size.

Porto Cabello and **Coro Coffees** also largely consumed, vary in the bean from medium to small, and from dark to pale green. They are classed as Mild Coffee, but their liquor develops **good strength** as well as flavor.

It has been said by some that much of the two types just mentioned hardly compares favorably with **Santos Coffee.** In the writer's opinion it at least takes a splendid **Santos** to compare favorably with them.

Among other varieties largely exported are **Carupano** and **Angostura.**

All of the **Maracaibo** types are **good blenders; the** higher **types** for **body** and rich full flavor, the **lesser types** add tone and flavor to many other Coffees.

CENTRAL AMERICA
Guatemala, Costa Rica, Salvador

The **finest** Central American **Coffee** is generally that from Guatemala, a Republic on the Pacific Coast, where cultivation is conducted on most modern lines. The best type of Guatemala Coffee is the **Coban,** a large shapely blue bean, producing a fine aromatic liquor; a type that drinks well alone, and makes a fine **blender** for **either lighter** or heavier types.

Coban Coffees grow in a mountainous region, near the town of Coban, and is usually transported on mule back over the mountain passes, and the bags are frequently not more than half the ordinary size.

While many **Guatemala** Coffees have **more style** than body, there are, however, many of them of **good strength** and rich flavor, and the **Coffees** from the **Coban** district rank with the **best** Coffees in the world.

The cultivation of Coffee in Guatemala began shortly after the middle of the last century. To-day Coffee is the most important product of Guatemala.

Prior to the European War two-thirds of the production went to Germany, where it commanded high prices. Of late, however, exports to the United States have increased considerably. and Guatemala Coffee is **rapidly growing in favor in** this country.

THE COFFEE PRODUCING DISTRICTS

As is the case with most producing countries, some districts in Guatemala produce more desirable Coffee than others. Each lot must be tested on its own merits. The Coban district produces a Coffee of exceptional merit, grown at an altitude of from 3,500 to 5,000 feet. Coban Coffees **rank** among the **finest Coffees** in the world. The Coban crop is comparatively small, however. Coffees from the **Antigua** district also are of **particularly high grade.** Numerous other sections produce Coffees considerably above the average. Costa Cuca is the most productive district.

The Coffee growing districts of Guatemala, named in the order of their production, are as follows: Costa Cuca, Costa Grande, Barberena, Tumbador, Coban, Costa de Cusho, Chicacao, Holhnitz, Pochuta Malacatan, San Marcos, Chuva, Escuintla San Vicente, Pacaya, Antigua, Moran, Amatitlan, Palmar and Motagua.

HOW TO USE GUATEMALA COFFEE

Guatemala Coffees are particularly useful for blending purposes, giving satisfactory character to high combinations. Those grown in the higher altitudes are heavy bodied, winey drinking Coffees, and blend well with **Javas, Bourbon Santos,** and **Maracaibos.** The Guatemalas grown in the lower altitudes do not possess the same heavy bodied winey drinking qualities, **but are smoother,** and when mixed with **Bogotas** or fine **Costa Ricas,** not alone materially enhance the drinking quality but lend a pleasing appearance to the blend. The lower grown Coffees should be roasted a light cinnamon color for best results, while the high grown, hard bean Coffees should be roasted along the same lines as **Bogota, Coatepec Mexicans,** or other choice Coffees of that character.

While there are many differences of opinion as to what constitutes the most desirable Coffee from the viewpoint of the consumer, straight Guatemala Coffee grown in the medium altitudes, or, say, from 3,000 to 4,000 feet above sea level, makes a most satisfactory out-turn. A Roaster in the West, who had a small retail stand in a market, and who sold for his best quality only straight Guatemala Coffee, met with such gratifying results that he gradually enlarged to a wholesale distribution, with the result that today he is using more than 5,000 bags yearly, advertising and selling only Guatemala Coffee.

CHARACTERISTICS OF GUATEMALA COFFEES

Guatemala leads, in Central America, in production with a crop averaging 750,000 bags, of which, normally, about one-third comes to the United States. They are very stylish Coffees, and have waxy, bluish bean, which, in roasting, split open with white centers. This enables them to com-

mand a high price, especially in European markets, but they are thin in body and are used
chiefly for their style. A small proportion of really
meritorious Coffees are produced in the mountainous districts of Coban and Antigua, at an altitude
of from 3,500 to 5,000 feet. The Cobans are grown
so near the frost line that they often contain
many frosted and blighted beans, to the detriment
of their style, but they have a fine, winey character, and possess body so heavy that it borders on
bitterness. They are especially fine for blending.
Less than 2,500 bags are imported annually. It has
been said that a hundred times more Cobans are
sold than are produced. The Antiguas are small-
ish, flinty bean Coffees, from a district about a
thousand feet lower. They are not so heavy in
body as the Cobans, but are flavory and winey, and
find favor upon the Pacific Coast, where some
15,000 to 20,000 bags are received.

Costa Rica: Perhaps equally as important is the
output of Costa Rica, the most Southern of the
five Central American Republics, producing one of
the finest Coffees in the world. (However, the
United States gets so little, if any, of the high type
Costa Rica Coffees, and so many of the poorer
types, that Costa Rica Coffee is not overly popular
here.) The high type Costa Rica is of heavy body
and sharply winey, and are best adapted for blending. Europe has nearly always paid a premium
on these, especially the larger bean Coffees.

The raw bean averages large and handsome, and
roasts to excellent advantage; however, the bulk
of the best grades go to Europe generally, and
many shipments of the lower qualities sent to the
United States give a liquor somewhat bitter or
brackish, and not very desirable.

About the year 1720 the first Coffee plants were
grown by the French Colonizers in the Island of
Martinique. From there they distributed seeds to
Jamaica and the other Islands of the West Indies

about 1725, and to **Rio de Janeiro,** also the other **Spanish** colonies of **Central** and **South America,** in 1770.

The same tree produces beans of different shapes and sizes, constituting four grades, namely: **Caracole** (shell shape), first, second, and third.

The proportion is approximately 5% **Caracole,** 25% first, 45% second, and 25% third.

The **Caracole** is so called (in this section) because the bean is somewhat the shape of the small shell ('Spanish Caracol snail).

The **European War,** which closed the **German** markets, has forced **Costa Rica** to look for new **Coffee** customers, and its product is again becoming more of a factor in the **North American** market, where an intelligent propaganda, combined with the **merits** of the article, is creating a greater consumer demand for it.

The price paid for the better grades of **Costa Rica** Coffees have always ranked among the high-est **paid** for any **Central American Coffees.**

The higher tableland (mesa central) of **Costa Rica** is admirably suited in the way of **soil** and **climatic conditions** for the production of a high-grade Coffee, which is highly prized in the markets of Europe, especially in Great Britain.

COSTA RICAS UNSURPASSED FOR BLENDING

Costa Rica's production of 200,000 bags is smaller than it was a half century ago. The fine **grades** are grown in the districts of **Cartago, San Jose, Alajuela** and **Grecia,** at altitudes of from 4,000 to 6,000 feet. These are characterized by their rich body and fine flavor, and are often so sharply **winey, that if used straight would sour the cream.** For blending, the Highland Coffees of **Costa Rica are surpassed by none of the world's growth, but,** unfortunately, Europe overbids us from 2 to 3 cents per pound, so that the 30,000 bags received in the United States are mainly the small bean separations and low grades.

The Salvador bean is generally of medium size, and, in best grades, is well developed, heavy and greyish yellow; the liquor is just fairly strong, with only a moderate flavor.

The poorer grades are very uneven and broken, and the liquor weak. The better grades do quite well as a blender with the heavier Coffees, say, with a Mexican, Guatemalan, or like types.

The land in Salvador is well adapted to the growth of Coffee. The mountain sides and high hills give the exact temperature needed, and of late years, since the intelligent use of fertilizers has been found to give results, well repaying the cost. Old plantations that were producing little before, have since made remarkable strides to the fore.

SALVADOR COFFEE MARKET CHIEFLY IN EUROPE

The Salvador crop of 300,000 bags is mainly marketed in Europe. San Francisco receives some 85,000 bags, which are consumed on the Pacific Coast. The proportion of mountain Coffees is small, and those that are washed rule about ¾ cent below Guatemalas of equal grade, which growth they resemble. The crop is principally the naturals, which are large bean and of fair average roast. There are about 220,000 acres of Coffee trees in Salvador.

Nicaragua closely resembles the medium grades of Salvador, possibly a little stronger, at least more pungent. Not a good individual drinker but useful in building around rank types, e. g. not bad with Rios or even Liberians, and prove quite a modifier.

Honduras produces a yellow, heavy bean of attractive appearance. The liquor is smooth and pleasing, but rather weak and frequently marked with a cocoa odor.

Panama has not yet established any high records, but the quality of the product has been considerably improved in recent years.

MEXICO

Mexican Coffee is roughly divided into "washed" and "unwashed", the former being the choicer. All green Coffees are either "washed" or "natural" (unwashed) so you may know that a "washed" Mexican or a "natural" Nicaragua means just that.

Usually "unwashed" Coffees show a dark spermodern or "silver skin" in the longitudinal cleft or center of the flat side of the bean when roasted. A "washed" Coffee generally shows a clean, light, bright to whitish center.

The bulk of the export formerly went to France, but the United States receipts have grown largely in recent years.

Mexican Coffees have won an important place with the American trade, both on account of the liberal supply and because the highland Coffees rank with the best produced in the world. They have full, rich body and a fine winey "bouquet" or aroma surpassed by none. The United States consumes more than a third of the annual crop, which reaches nearly 400,000 bags. This production is mainly from a small area of some 200 miles, which is situated nearly the same distance inland from Vera Cruz. About 10% of the importation are the West Francisco.

COATEPEC COFFEES AMONG THE WORLD'S BEST

The finest Mexicans are produced in the district of Coatepec (Co-at-e-pee), at an altitude of from 3,000 to 4,000 feet. The combination of climatic condition, altitude and the rich volcanic soil gives a quality which places these in the front rank with the world's best Coffees. When aged for a year in the Mexican climate, their winey character is tempered, and they so mellow that they indeed become perfection. Unfortunately, the high rate of interest prohibit their being held for this purpose, and, ordinarily, they are rushed to the market as soon as they can be harvested and prepared for shipment. Many other Mexican Coffees are marketed under the name Coatepec.

CORDOBA COFFEES ARE BEAUTIFUL ROASTERS

Some fine Coffees are raised from 500 to 1,000 feet lower in the adjoining districts of Jalapa (Ha-lap-pa). The district of chief production is Cordova, which is on the southern side of the volcano. These are very stylish Coffees, especially beautiful roasters, but they are thin in body, and do not compare with those first described. The districts of Orizaba and Huatusco (Wha-too-co) adjoin. The Coffees from the former resemble medium grade Cordobas. Some of the higher growths in the latter district are of fair cup quality.

The two "fanciest" commercial types of Mexican beans are the Coatepec ("Tepic") and Caracolillo, the latter being generally known as "Mexican Peaberry."

Coatepec or "Tepic", formerly known as "Mexican Mocha", is said to be grown from a later introduction of the Arabian shrub, so carefully cultivated that some judges consider the product fully equal (?) in quality to that of the parent plant. The bean is small, hard and of a steel-blue color, making a creamy, aromatic liquor. Very little of this variety is exported, local consumers taking nearly all the crop. These Coffees are really most wonderful when you get the best washed type. The writer in many instances has found them almost identical with good Bogotas.

43

NATURAL MEXICANS LIMITED TO LOW GRADES

Sierras and Tampicos are low growth, and, being "woody", are used for low-grade purposes. High-growth Coffees improve with age, while in many cases low-growths become woody and punky. The shipment of natural Mexicans has fallen off until they are limited to the cheaper grades. Many low-growths are "hidey", due to the excessive fermentation explained in the preceding talk. Occasionally sour beans are found in even fancy Mexicans, so that care must be used in selection. The fine Mexicans are valuable for adding "meat" and richness to fancy blends, as well as flavor and their winey character.

Caracolillo is a variety almost unique. As already noted, "Pea-berries" are found to some extent in all Coffee bean crop, but the shrubs from which the Caracolillo product is obtained bear it almost exclusively.

After these two types, which do not effect the general market, come Oaxaca, Cordoba, Coatepec, Colima, etc.

The Oaxaca (War-har-kar) bean is large and well developed, blue in color when new, but becoming whiter as it ages, the liquor is strong, rich and fragrant, and notwithstanding the high tribute paid the Tepic type, the Oaxaca Coffees are the leading Mexican growth and the sharpest, winey flavor of all other Mexican Coffees, and has good body; they come "washed" and "unwashed," the former being termed "Pluma," and the latter being known simply as Oaxaca.

Cordoba is sometimes styled "Mexican Jack" The bean is large and yellow, and the liquor is rich and full, resembling a fine Maracaibo or a medium "Java."

The Coatepec bean is large, well developed and more winey than most types.

44

Colima is a medium sized bean, flat, fairly well developed, and with liquor pleasing in flavor and moderately rich.

Small quantities come also from **Tuxpam,** and several **lowland** districts, but the quality is usually **inferior**

Taken as a whole, **Mexican** Coffees are very fine Coffees, particularly useful in **blending.**

JAVA AND OTHER DUTCH EAST INDIAN ISLANDS

The **Dutch East Indies,** especially the Islands of **Java, Sumatra** and **Celebes,** are famous as the largest exporters of fine Coffees. They are best known to the lay public by the name of the Island of **Java,** the most populous of the group and the central point of **Dutch** commercial activity, but the greater part of the East Indian Coffee consumed in the **United States** is of **Sumatra** growth. That from **Celebes** is generally **rated** the **highest** in **European** markets.

Other countries produce in certain sections, beans as choice as the very best **"Java",** but the quantities they can export are comparatively unimportant.

The greater output of the Dutch East Indies is partly due to the natural **adaptability** of soil and climate, and partly to the systematic **cultivation** by native inhabitants under the rule of **Holland.** In spite of governmental care, there is, however, much variation in the beans grown; a considerable quantity of those exported do not deserve the reputation the "Javas" have earned.

Only Coffees grown on the Island of **Java** can be labeled **Java** in the **United States.**

Java Coffee was originally of the **Coffee Arabica** variety, but now the **Liberian** and **Robusta** varieties are also grown on the Island. The **Java** bean takes on a **rusty brown** color as it **ages;** it also becomes more **mellow** and **flavory.** However, this last may be said of practically all Coffees. A bluish-green is the original fresh color of **Javas**. The bean is large, full, well formed, and are classed among the very best individual drinkers, and very superior blenders.

East Indian Coffees are in this country principally graded by color—"Brown", "Yellow" and "Pale"; the darker beans bringing the higher price.

This discrimination was originally founded on the fact that some of the choicest varieties of "Java" beans become at the same time browner in color and more mellow and pleasing in flavor, in storage and transport, being in the former respect entirely unique.

The distinction is not fundamentally accurate, as some of the light bean varieties are better than many of the dark types. In Europe the yellow colored beans are preferred. When fresh, all East Indian Coffees are light sea-green, or blue-green.

Dutch East Indian Coffees, other than those grown on the Island of Java itself, are now generally described in trade and government circles as Dutch East Indian, or by trade titles, or by districts, as, Ankola, Padang, Mandheling, Corinche, Timor, Kroe, etc. The title "Government" is sometimes applied as a distinguishing title to Coffee produced on plantations operated under government supervision, as are all old and many of the new plantations.

The title "Old Government Java" was at one time a name to conjure with, for, as first employed, it applied to beans that had been held, sometimes for considerable periods, in the government storehouses. Until a few years ago, nearly all the produce of the Dutch East Indies was sold by quarterly Government auction, and any goods for which the upset price was not bid, were held in the warehouses to await an improvement in market demands, the result being in many cases an improvement also in the Coffees, Spices, etc., by the opportunity thus given them to mature under the best possible condition. The term long ago, though, deteriorated into a practically meaningless trade title from being applied indiscriminately to any brown East Indian Coffee, irrespecttive of growth or quality, and it is now "out of date", as the government auctions were discontinued in June, 1909, present sales being by contracts with firms or individuals.

"Plantation" or "private growth" Coffees are those raised on plantations owned and operated by individuals in contra-distinction to those under government supervision. Some are of very high quality.

"Blue-bean Java" is a title occasionally applied to W. I. P. or "washed" East Indian.

"Liberian Java" (often called "African Java") is that grown from shrubs of Liberian species. Its quality is usually inferior to the Arabian bean varieties; it seems unnecessary to say this, however, if one stops to compare the two original types, Arabian and Liberian. The former the classiest Coffee, known for excellent flavor; the latter of the most pronounced characteristic, of such unusual strength and distinctiveness as to closely approach rankness.

Padang Coffees get their name from the principal shipping port of the Island of Sumatra, on Sumatra's West Coast, which was at one time the center of the Dutch Government's Coffee trade. Many Coffees produced on the Island come from this port, and are often called Padang. Among them, called by their district names, are: Boekit Gompong, Painam, Interior, Ayer-Bangies, Ankola, Mandheling, Soerian, Loeboe, Rayamerapi and Samarang.

Mendheling Coffee gets its name from the Mandheling district of Sumatra's West Coast. This Coffee commands the highest price of any in the world (Mocha possibly excepted), and many authorities consider it the very finest grown. It is bought and sold even in the United States as "Mandheling Java". This is a misnomer, for it is strictly a **Sumatra** and **not** a **Java**, according to **our** standards, that is, Java Coffee must come from the Island of **Java**.

Corinche: One of the fine grades of **Dutch East Indian** Coffees, securing its name from the town of **Corinche**, is Southwest **Sumatra**, Southeast of **Padang**.

Timor: A comparatively small amount of this Coffee is grown on the Timor Island of the **Timor Archipelago East** of the **Sumba** Islands and **North** of Australia. This is a good quality Coffee.

SUMATRAS SUPERIOR TO JAVAS

As a matter of fact, the true **Java** does not compare even favorably with **Sumatras** in quality, with the exception of the choicest. **Javas** are grassy, greenish, brashy and thin liquored. Their principal value consists in the **fact** that **they are Javas.** Javas give the largest production, but these are not the really fine Coffees. The famous **Mandheling** and **Ankola** districts are located in **Sumatra**, also the districts of **Corinche**, Padang and **Kroe**. The **Ayer-Bangies**, **Palembangs** and **Boengies** are hardly note-worthy, as the supply has become limited.

The **prime** value of **East Indies** Coffees is in their **smooth, heavy body:** the fancies possessing an almost **syrupy richness.** Their characteristics are found to quite an extent in choice old **Bucaramangas**, and occasionally in certain fancy old **Maracaibos.** These are frequently used as substitutes, or in conjunction with **East Indian** Coffees, both because they reach the mark and reduce the cost.

Sumatra Coffee is produced on the island of that name in the **Dutch East Indies.** It comprises the principal part of the production in the Islands, and, in fact, is the finest of these growths.

48

Ankola Coffee is produced in the Ankola district in the Island of Sumatra, and is considered one of the finest Coffees grown. It has a very heavy body and delicate, rich flavor. Ankolas are classed close to Mandhelings, and, although not so heavy in body, their characteristics are similar. They are sometimes given the preference because of their large, regular bean and fine roasting qualities. Corinches, which are now received in limited quantity, are often used in place of Ankolas, which Coffees they closely resemble. They range from 1 to 2 cents under Ankolas in price. Padang is Sumatra's chief seaport, and this name is sometimes applied to Mandhelings, Ankolas, Corinches and interiors.

Kroe: A medium grade East India Coffee grown in the district of the same name, and is shipped from Port Kroe on the Southwest Coast of the Island of Sumatra.

KROES ARE GOOD ROASTERS AND BLENDERS

The Coffees from the Island of Timor are classed below Padangs, being inferior in bean and style. Kroes are better known and more widely used because of their liberal supply, which also influences their price. They are good roasters and blenders, usually quite uniform in bean.

Samarang Coffee is generally a yellowish-green color in the bean, and light and thin in cup quality. Grown on the North Coast of the Island of Java and is named after a Seaport town.

ROBUSTA COFFEE

Coffee Laurentii or Robusta Coffee is a species discovered growing wild in the Congo by Emil Laurent. A Brussels horticultural firm took it up, commercially designated it Robusta. It is now being extensively cultivated in Java and is sometimes called **Robusta Java.** This Coffee is in the experimental stage, and has very little merit in the cup, excepting a type well aged and brought to a dark chocolate roast; even then the liquor is light, with little or no flavor, but it is particularly clean and free from imperfections, therefore grading high; it is practically neutral and is used considerably as a filler. Much attention has been given this Coffee because its tree is a more hardy variety than most other Coffee trees.

The Coffee Exchange of the City of New York prohibited the delivery of this growth of Coffee on **Exchange contracts** after March 1, 1913.

Batavia is the Capital of the Dutch East Indian Colony of Java, and is the principal market for Coffee grown in that Island. The port of **Batavia** is **Tandjong, Priok.**

ARABIA—MOCHA

Mocha, a former important Coffee port on the **Red Sea, Arabia.** All the Coffee produced in Arabia is known by the name "Mocha," though no Coffee was ever grown in Mocha, which is only a shipping town surrounded by deserts, and not today even an important shipping point, as the opening of the Suez Canal transferred nearly all the traffic to the ports of **Aden and Hodeida.** The **Port** of Mocha was closed by a sand bar nearly a hundred years ago, and **Coffee** has since been shipped by the way of Aden.

The plantations are located in the interior of the **Yemen** district, with **Sana** as the center of cultivation. Right at this point is where the finest Arabian Coffee is grown, but it is never exported. The methods of cultivation, harvesting and curing are most primitive. The berries are **not picked as in other countries,** but are **permitted** to ripen on the trees, after which they fall naturally and are allowed to dry in the cherry.

THE FOUR GRADES OF MOCHA

There are four grades of Mocha, viz: Grade No. 1, which contains only perfect berries and is absolutely free from dust. Grade No. 1-A, containing perfect berries but in which a little dust may be found. Grade No. 2, containing some broken Coffee and "quakers," and Grade No. 3, in which may be found a much heavier percentage of both "broken" and "quakers," as well as some dust.

The Coffee is packed in fiber bundles or "bales," weighing about 160 pounds each. Two or four pockets to every bale.

Mocha beans are exceedingly small, hard and round, irregular in form and size, olive green in color, shading off to pale yellow.

PECULIAR CHARACTERISTICS OF MOCHA COFFEE

Mocha Coffee has a peculiar winey character, found in no other Coffee, and a heavy body. The roast is poor and irregular, showing up a large quantity of "quakers," particularly in the lowest grades. The "quakers" apparently do not materially affect the cup character. It is a particularly good Coffee to use in blending on account of its winey character. The best known blends are those made in combination with various growths of the Dutch East Indies, but the Coffee is acceptable when used with any of the fancy washed types. As a straight beverage it is found pleasing, and when made as a heavy after-dinner Coffee is especially good.

The best Arabian—and the true "Mocha," is that from the province of Yemen. The most surprising point in connection with its cultivation is that though the Coffee shrub requires in other countries rich soil and favorable conditions to produce an acceptable crop, here in Arabia, some of the choicest Coffee in the world comes from stunted shrubs growing in hot, sandy, stony mountainside gardens. All conditions, climate and soil seem to be against the shrubs best growth, but by the way of recompense it receives the most careful and painstaking human attention The gardens are arranged on rocky terraces, one above the other, and are irrigated from large reservoirs of spring water placed above the highest.

There are two main crops during the year. The berries, instead of being picked, are allowed to ripen until they fall. They are then carefully gathered up, dried, hulled and cleaned with scrupulous exactness. The separation of the finest "Mocha" beans by growers and merchants is in itself a study of infinite detail; they are assorted into a perfect graduation of sizes and qualities.

The true Yemen "Mocha" bean is very small, hard and round, regular in size in the best qualities: Olive-green when new and a rich semi-transparent yellowish when aged. Its odor when fresh roasted is characteristic, and the liquor is creamy, rich, rather heavy, a little winey and extremely aromatic and fragrant.

"Tehama'" Arabian Coffee—that from the province of Tehama, is distinctly inferior to Yemen. The bean is about the same size, but it is immature in appearance and often mixed with fragments of hull, etc., its flavor is quite second rate when drunk alone, unless used as an extra heavy after-dinner Coffee, but it imparts a pleasing fragrance and delicacy when blended with a good "Java," etc.

Abyssinian Coffee from the vicinity of Harrar and properly called "Harrar Coffee" was formerly shipped via Aden as long-berry "Mocha." It is of of the same color as the real "Mocha," but is longer and more pointed, and has a rank leathery odor. Harrar is the Capital and trade center of the District of Harrar in Southeastern Abyssinia, an Italian Protectorate, 6,000 feet above sea level.

This is the town from which long-berry Harrar Coffee (sometimes termed Abyssinian or Long-berry Mocha) is shipped, also Abyssinian Coffee grown in the neighborhood of Adis Abeba.

LONG-BERRY HARRAR

This Coffee is classified in two varieties, Harrar and Abyssinian.

Harrar Coffee is grown principally in the Province of Harrar, near the City of the same name. This Coffee has a larger bean than Arabian Mocha, but is quite similar in appearance. In color it is a blue green, shading to yellow. The Coffee is usually graded as No. 1 or No. 2, depending upon the size and color of the bean.

From the City of Harrar the Coffee is transported on mules to Dire-Daoua, and from there forwarded to Djibouti. It is then taken across the Red Sea in small boats to the English port of Aden, whence it is transshipped to all parts of the world.

ABYSSINIAN COFFEE GROWS UNCULTIVATED

The other variety is known as Abyssinian. It grows in a wild state in the province west of Harrar, principally in the Kaffa district, around Adis Abba and north of that city. The trees are permitted to grow in a wild, uncultivated condition, the berries being picked from the ground. This Coffee is not graded, contains many imperfections and is of a dark-gray color. Little, if any, of this particular type reaches this country.

Prior to the passage of the Food and Drugs Act, Harrar Coffee was known as Long-Berry Mocha, to distinguish it from the Arabian Coffee, which, as a rule, is a shorter, smaller bean.

The Arabian product, to which had been given the term Mocha, from the port of shipment, being, as a rule, superior to Harrar Coffee, the latter finally assumed the title Long-berry Mocha, thereby commanding a, higher price. As long as the trade could use it as Mocha Coffee it was in fair demand, for the reason that it could usually be secured at a cent to a cent and a half below the prevailing price of the genuine Arabian Mocha.

In the cup the character is, similar to the Arabian product, but usually not as delicate, although at times shipments of Harrar Coffee have been received that have been found to be superior to some of the Mocha Coffee on the market.

Since the passage of the Food and Drugs Act, the demand for Harrar Coffee has decreased, owing to the fact that it cannot be offered to the trade in combination with Java and a blend of Java and Mocha.

Genuine "Mocha" is sometimes called "short-berry" "Mocha"; this is really superfluous, as there is no other kind of Mocha Coffee, while most insignificant in appearance it is considered the finest type of Coffee known. It is most excellent in blends, and used almost entirely for this purpose. Its great richness and its extreme aromatic flavor renders it more suitable as a blender than an individual drinker.

Sanani is a high grade short berry Arabian (Mocha) Coffee, coming from the district around Sana Yemen.

WEST INDIAN COFFEE

The West Indian Islands produce a large quantity of excellent Coffee, but the bulk of the finest grades is exported to Europe, as better prices can generally be obtained there than in this market. The greater part of the supply shipped to this country comes from the British West Indies, principally from Jamaica and Haiti, with small quantities from Santo Domingo, Cuba and the Dutch West Indies.

The best Jamaica Coffee, known as "Blue Mountain," is a bean of fair size, attractive in appearance and bluish color, making a full, rich, fragrant
liquor. It is sometimes called Blue Mountain Jamaica and grown in the Jamaica district. But
"Plain-Grown," the variety chiefly imported, is a
much Inferior grade. The bean, large, whitish,
and flat, is generally "hully" and the liquor is
strong and rather rank or "grassy" in flavor. It
is used almost exclusively for blending with beans
of other varieties.

Haitian and Santo Domingo beans are large, flat
and whitish. Their appearance is spoiled by
crude preparation, which leaves them "hully" and
includes broken beans, stems, etc. Their liquor
is not unpleasant, but lacks body, in fact is hardly considered good.

Santo Domingo, Capital of the Dominican Republic on the Island of Haiti and lends the name
Santo Domingo to Coffee, a Coffee as a rule very
carelessly prepared, hence the average quality is
very poor.

The best Cuban grades come from the Guanta-
namo, Alquizar and Marcos districts and the Sierra Maestra plantations. The beans are large and
whitish, and rather rounded on the flat side. They
are generally good cuppers.

Porto Rico produces very fine Coffee, the beans
regular and well formed, usually yellow to greenish in color and very stylish. The best of this
variety "washed" commands a good premium in
European markets, and the bean of this grade is
a large handsome bluish-green, and a very stylish
roaster.

CEYLON AND INDIA

Coffee-growing in Ceylon reached its height in
1890; since then its production has steadily de-
clined, the people turning their attention more
extensively to tea and rubber.

There are several distinct varieties of **Ceylon Coffees**, as follows:: **"Native"**, grown in the lowlands, a large, flat, white bean of inferior cup quality. **"Plantation"**, the product of carefully cultivated planations, the bean large, of light-bluish to a greenish tint, well developed and very regular, giving a liquor which is smooth, rich and aromatic.

"Liberian-Ceylon", a hybrid" of the **Liberian** species; the bean smaller and paler than the **parent** variety, and the liquor less strong, producing a smooth cup of pleasing flavor.

"Ceylon-Mocha", a small bean, very even and uniform, generally obtained by separating from the regular "plantation" crop. Both in appearance and in the cup it resembles the genuine **"Mocha"**

The **two best-known** varieties of **Indian Coffees** are **Malabar**, a small, hard bean of most **excellent** quality, used locally largely for **blending** and for the best trade.

"Mysore", a large, bluish-green bean, roasting well and producing a rich, strong liquor, resembling **Java** quite a little.

ECUADOR (GUAYAQUILS)

Coffees from **Ecuador** are generally known as **Guayaquils**, from the port of that name. The beans run from medium to large. They are firmly uniform in appearance, roast well and give off a full, aromatic liquor. The United States gets quite a lot of **Ecuador** Coffee.

PHILIPPINES

The Coffee plant waas introduced into the Philippine Islands by the Spanish missionaries from **Java**, about 1740. It was produced there for export for many years, but the plant has been nearly exterminated by various pests and insects, and the crop is not so large nor so good as it once was.

The Coffee industry is improving through improved cultivation and more proper handling, and it is only a question of time when that country will fill an important position in the Coffee world, the Soil and climatic conditions being admirably suited to Coffee culture.

In spite of very inferior preparation and scanty attention, the better grades are held in high esteem in the European markets, being recognized as very rich and flavory types.

The beans are generally classed as Luzon, Manila and Zamboanga, the two latter from shipping ports, the former from the Luzon district.

Luzon is a small bean, hard and attractive when properly cleaned and prepared (which is seldom), and ranks high.

The Manila bean is medium size, regular in shape, and pale green in color, with fine aromatic liquor. It comes principally from the districts of Cavite, Batangas, La Laguna and the immediate vicinity.

Zamboanga, from the Southern Islands, is the poorest grade. The beans are large, yellowish and rather flabby, the liquor is coarse, brackish and weak.

HAWAII

The Konos are perhaps the best Hawaiian production in Coffees. Kono Coffee beans are medium to large, well formed, stylish lookers, good healthy green, fine attractive roasters, rich, very flavory and of good strength; excellent blenders; classy cuppers.

The Coffee plant is cultivated in many of the Pacific Islands: the Islands of Guinea, Fiji, the Friendly and Samoan groups.

In the Hawaiian Islands, the production has reached considerable proportions, the production being of a very classy character as a rule.

In addition to the countries previously mentioned, there are a number of other countries which would help materially in raising the total production. Some of these are fine quality and good types, but the imports into the **United States** are **not** sufficient in volume to affect the **market conditions.**

Green Coffee is received in the United States in **bags, mats** and **bales. Bags** from Brazil usually weigh about 1'35 pounds. **Bags** from other countries weigh more as a rule, sometimes weighing more than 200 pounds, particularly **Liberian Coffee.** Ordinarily, however, a **bag** of Coffee will rarely weigh more than 150 pounds. All countries ship their **green coffee** in **bags,** excepting **Arabia,** which produces only Mocha and that is shipped in bales weighing usually 160 pounds net. Each **bale** contains either **two** or four "pockets" of Coffee. **Mats** or fibre bags are used in the shipment of **Kroes** and other **East Indian Coffees;** however, all Coffee, excepting **Mocha,** is almost universally shipped in **bags. Mats** are similar to bales, only they usually have **two pockets** to the bag, and the **mat** rarely ever holds more than 60 pounds, while the Mocha **bale** holds 160 pounds.

Caffeine: The stimulating principle of Coffee. It is chemically identical to the **theine** of **Tea, Cola,** etc.

COFFEE IMPORTS, PRICE AND CONSUMPTION
Five Year Averages—1851-1914

Period	Net Imports Quantity Pounds	Net Imports Value Dollars	Import Price per Lb. Cents	Per Capita Con- sumption Pounds
1851-55....	168,200,000	13,800,000	8.24	6.57
1856-60....	208,700,000	19,900,000	9.60	7.03
1861-65....	115,500,000	12,500,000	10.70	3.48
1866-70....	214,500,000	22,200,000	10.44	5.78
1871-75....	297,500,000	42,900,000	14.52	7.14
1876-80....	350,500,000	52,300,000	15.14	7.34
1881-85....	477,000,000	44,700,000	9.64	8.86
1886-90....	499,500,000	60,200,000	12.26	8.33
1891-95....	576,400,000	96,700,000	16.82	8.72
1896-00....	739,800,000	65,400,000	9.28	10.10
1901-05....	943,000,000	66,200,000	7.10	11.65
1906-10....	916,300,000	72,100,000	7.90	10.30
1911-14....	900,400,000	108,600,000	12.12	9.35

AN EMINENT PHYSICIAN SAYS.

Coffee is a food, a whip, a fertilizer, a heat-maker, a true stimulant and thirst-quencher

Roasted Coffee in bulk contains little or no moisture, but over 13% of fat and oil. About 2% of sweet stuff, such as sugar and dextrin are in it, as well as 50% of pulp and pitch. About 5% of mineral fertilizer is present and nearly 1% of the powerful stimulant, Caffeine.

Albumen is the real food in Coffee, and it occurs in quantities as large as 12%.

Of course, a cup of Coffee has a lot of water in addition to the other constituents, but this, together with the heat, makes Coffee all the more easily digested.

Other than the oils, fats, albumens, caramel, sugar and sweets in Coffee, its intrinsic distinction is the wonderful alkaloid, Caffeine. This strange drug in one-grain doses adds to human endurance, muscular exertion, mental efficiency and physiological effort in a most extraordinary way.

"In all our private and hospital experience, we have never encountered an instance in which dyspepsia, nervousness, or any other ailment was reasonably attributable to the moderate and habitual use of Coffee as a beverage. It is true that hundreds of mortals deny themselves this boon, because of some fancied or educated fear that it isn't good for them. But we are speaking of facts now, and not popular delusions. A good many nervous and sickly people would be better off if they would take a cup of Coffee—good Coffee—for breakfast."

WHEN COFFEE IS A FOOD DRINK

Coffee, as the analysis will show, might be regarded as a fairly nourishing food, if taken directly with very little water, but since the drink is usually prepared by making an infusion of about two ounces to a pint of water, it will be seen that Coffee itself has only a slight nutriment value. Nevertheless, the addition of sugar and milk makes it valuable as a food. The food value of the raw berry, as eaten by the Arabs, is likewise dubious, for here the injection of such large amounts of caffeine into the system would certainly counteract any tissue-building effect the other constituents of the bean might have. A Coffee infusion, by the way, contains about 70-90% of the total caffeine of the berry after grounds have settled out. The accompanying figures show the number of calories obtained from one portion of the various foods as they are served in Child's Restaurants, and what the cost would be if the daily normal requirements of 2,500 calories were furnished entirely by that article.

CALORIES IN FOODS AND THEIR COST

	Calories in One Portion.	Cost in 2,500 Calories
Coffee	195.5	$.64
Cocoa	247.5	50
Milk	145.3	86
Cake	200-300.	40-.60
Toast	150.	.83
Soup	75-100.	2.50-3.33

It will be seen from these figures that the cup of Coffee provides a source of nutrition that is very reasonable in price, and that, compared with milk and soup, is quite an inexpensive food. This, in addition to the fact that it possesses stimulating properties and a delightful flavor and taste, should recommend it as a beverage once more to all who are interested in the scientific and economical planning of the dietary man.

ROASTING, BLENDING, CARE, ETC.

Next in importance to following and properly combining cup characteristics is uniformity of roasts. If too light, the bean is not fully developed, and the fibre cells not expanded for the release of the volatile oils, whereas if roasting is carried too far, the aroma and winey character are reduced or destroyed, the oils are "started" and partly driven off, the Coffee soon "sweats," becomes rancid, tough and hard to grind. To the frequent question, which is best, light or dark roasts,—ask the inquirer whether he prefers under-ripe fruit or that which is over-ripe. For normal distribution there is one proper degree of roast—rich cinnamon brown. At this point full development of both bean and cup characteristics are gained. A dark roast produces only bitterness, and bitterness is not body.

Coffees for soon consumption stand the full cinnamon limit, but those for distribution over a wide area, where they sometimes stand in grocers' stocks for weeks before being placed in consumption, are better preserved when roasted a shade lighter, as deterioration is rapid in full roasted Coffee. In making color comparisons, the Coffee should be finely ground and a spoonful of each placed upon glass over blue paper. They may be flattened, squared and edged, like the adjoining squares of a checker-board. With one's back to the light and the, Coffees held almost to the level of the eyes, even half or quarter shade variations may readily be distinguished.

It is a growing belief that in roasts of shorter duration, the largest percentage of the aromatic properties are retained. A slow roast has the effect of baking and does not give full development; also slow roasts seldom produce bright roasts and they usually make the Coffee hard instead of brittle, even when the color standard has been attained. While Coffees of widely varying degrees of moisture require somewhat different treatment, the concensus of opinion is that the best results are from a slower fire at the beginning, until some of the moisture has been driven off, when the stronger application of heat may be given for development. An intense heat in the beginning often results in "tipping," charring the little germ at the end, the most sensitive part of the bean.

Scorched beans are due to their being caught at some point in the cylinder, often in a bent flange. Burning on one face, sometimes called "kissing the cheeks" is caused by the too rapid revolution of the cylinder, so that some of the Coffee "carries over." According to the best practice, crowding of cylinders is avoided, many roasters making it a rule not to exceed 90 per cent of their rated capacity. Those operating gas roasters may effect a fuel economy by running a low grade Coffee in the cylinder after the last roast has been drawn and the gas extinguished; five minutes revolution absorbs the heat and drives off a proportion of moisture. The Coffee, which may then be left in the cylinder is warming up. Double roasting brightens a roast, but it is to the detriment of the cup quality. A dull roasting Coffee may be improved by revolving the green Coffee in a cylinder without heat for twenty minutes, this having the effect of milling.

The use of a small amount of water upon roasts gives better control by checking the roast at the proper point—the crucial time of its greatest heat; also it **swells** and **brightens** the Coffee. While the addition of water is open to abuse, we believe but very few **roasters** have soaked their Coffees to offset the natural shrinkage three to four per cent. Such practice would result greatly to the detriment of the cup quality.

ROASTING REQUIRES INTELLIGENCE AND STUDY

Do not take for granted **too** much of **what I** or **anyone** else may tell you. Try for yourself. While I will tell you what is good with me, do not forget that Coffee must **be good before** it is **blended,** if it is going to be good after blending. You cannot buy your Coffees hit or miss and expect them to make a good blend. Study your Coffee and study your trade.

Always remember that there can be no set rules for roasting, as different Coffees require different handling. The man who roasts Coffee should be just as intelligent and just as responsible as the man who does the firm's bookkeeping. The bookkeeper can do all of his work by rule, but the roaster must use his own judgment, for he has no set rules to govern him.

It is not really **necessary** that the **roaster** should know how to blend, but if he is a **good blender** he is that much more **valuable** to his firm.

As to different blends, I will give a few that I know to be good, but, of course, I cannot lay down hard, fast rules that will apply to every section of the country, for I do not know what Coffees cost, laid down in all stores, or what are the demands of the trade in every place. That is something which each blender must learn for himself.

I use very few Rios in any of my blends, as there are so few people who like that strong Rio flavor, and it does not pay to carry a blend with Rio in it, although I carry a line of Rio to please the trade that calls for it.

For a good cheap Coffee, the best Santos you can afford generally gives the best satisfaction. For better, one-third Bogota and two-thirds of good Santos; or one-half Santos, one-fourth Bogota, one-fourth Guatemala; for still better, two-thirds Bogota, one-third Guatemala; or one-half Bogota, one-fourth Guatemala, one-fourth good Santos.

Of course, you can vary the grade and price of those blends by the amount of, or the price of the Santos you wish to use. Some Rio might be used in blends in certain territories. A good blend can be made with one-half Maracaibo, one-fourth Bogota, one-fourth Santos; or one-half Bogota, one-fourth Maracaibo, one-fourth Santos. But unless one is a pretty good judge of Coffee, I would advise not using Maracaibos in blends. A good Maracaibo is one of the best drinking Coffees grown, but they are hard to match, and after you have the line you think you want, you have to try every bag to be sure of it.

If the price permits, a good cup may be obtained through using one-half Bourbon with one-fourth each Maracaibo and low cost Bogota.

Stick to Bogota and Guatemala and Santos with Bogota, as the basis for best moderate price blends; they are bound to win out, as I think they are the best Coffees grown for blending purposes

EVERY BLEND SHOULD CONTAIN THREE COFFEES, OR MORE

In my judgment every blend should have at least three Coffees in it. In the event of not being able to match one of the Coffees the blender has been using, or that he can buy one at one-eight or one-quarter cent less a pound, would not be noticed in the blend; but when cheaper Coffee is bought it must not be used as a sample for the next lot, for one might be tempted to also shade that a little, and soon the good would be shaded out.

I do not think there is any Coffee that drinks as well by itself as when blended with some other Coffeee. Some blenders blend what are known to the trade as acid and non-acid Coffees. Others prefer to blend all acid Coffees, and still others prefer all non-acid Coffees. This is altogether a matter of taste, but when you start, blend up the different kinds and then decide on what you want and stick to it. Do not use acid Coffee one time and a non-acid the next. This is where two-thirds of the dealers are falling down today.

Take it for yourself: if you like a good, strong, winey Coffee, and someone gives you a cup of non-acid Coffee, you will say that the Coffee is no good, it is too flat. And if you like the non-acid better and get a cup of winey Coffee, you will say that is no good, as it is too rank or sour.

COFFEE AT THE "DRINKING POINT"

In buying your Coffees and trying them out in the cup, be very careful not to make up your mind too quickly, as sometimes a Coffee will taste fine when you first pour the boiling water upon it, but when it cools down to what I call the drinking point, it has flattened out to be practically no good, while on the other hand, the one that did not seem to be quite so good at the start holds its own or improves right through, until it becomes cold. I always give the preference to the Coffee that is best at the drinking point.

THE RANGE OF GRADES FOR BLENDING

The lowest grades of Brazil Coffee to be used for blending would be those known as Victorias. From this point we should pass on in the scale to Rio, from the low grades to the fancy old-crop golden Rio called for in certain sections of the country. Then there would follow the straight Santos Coffees, beginning with the low grades and running from this point to the medium grades, to be followed by the high-grade Santos types.

Under the head of Santos is the Coffee known as the **flat bean Santos**, and also those growths which, on account of appearance and **cup character,** are termed **Bourbon.** In **some sections** the flat beans would be **found desirable,** while in other sections the **Bourbon** Coffees would **be preferred.**

After the Brazils would come the mild Coffees, and in some instances these Coffees are **sold straight, rather than blended.** There is a certain percentage of the consuming trade that is better pleased with a straight Bogota Coffee than with a blend.

GROUPING COFFEES FOR BLENDING PURPOSES

When considering the various blends it will probably be more satisfactory if they are divided into groups. The first group would be the one containing the lowest-priced combinations, and naturally the greatest percentage of Santos. Therefore, the following suggestions will include blends of Coffees containing 50 per cent of Santos or Bourbon Santos as the dealer may find most acceptable in his location. They are simply to be taken as a basis from which the dealer may find it possible to work out acceptable brands for himself by varying the percentages of the Coffees used, as in his opinion the results warrant.

BLENDS OF SANTOS AND ONE OTHER COFFEE

The first series would naturally be those containing Santos with one other Coffee, as follows:

Santos and Maracaibo, Santos and Bucaramanga, Santos and Caracas, Santos and Bogota.

After this there would follow the combinations containing 50 per cent of either Santos or Bourbon Santos, with two other Coffees.

Santos, Bogota and Maracaibo; Santos, Bogota and Bucaramanga; Santos, Bogota and Guatemala; Santos, Bogota and Mexican.

BOGOTA AS THE BASIS FOR BLENDS

The next group would be a series of blends with Bogota as the basis. In many of these blends 50 per cent Bogota could be used, but in some, particularly those combinations with Dutch East Indian Coffees, the quantity of Bogota should be reduced. This series will run as follows:

Bogota and Bourbon; Bogota, washed Santos and Bourbon; Bogota and Guatemala; Bogota and Mexican; Bogota, Guatemala and Mexican; Bogota, washed Maracaibo and Guatemala; Bogota and East Indian; Bogota, Dutch East Indian and Mexican; Bogota, Dutch East Indian and Guatemala; Bogota, Dutch East Indian, washed Maracaibo and Guatemala; Bogota, Dutch East Indian and Mocha; Bogota, Dutch East Indian, Guatemala and Mocha.

The above would be followed by the various combinations that may be made up of Dutch East Indian with Mocha, and also the types of Coffee from the Island of Java with Mocha. These blends usually run from two-thirds to three-quarters Dutch East Indian of Java, the remainder being Mocha.

MOCHA HAS AN INDIVIDUALITY ALL ITS OWN

The character given to a brand of Coffee by the use of a percentage of Mocha opens up another line of blends. Many blends in years past have contained a very liberal percentage of Mocha, but it has been gradually replaced by Santos Coffees, because of their better appearance and lower price. There is an individuality to be found in a fine grade of Mocha that is not obtainable from Coffe grown anywhere outside of Arabia, so that blends containing reasonable percentage of Coffees from the Dutch East Indies and Arabia, together with fancy Mexican, Central American, or South American types, are among the finest obtainable.

Much of the **so-called** Coffee **blending** is nothing more nor less than **mixing** of Coffee together in order to obtain a fairly good-looking product at the **lowest possible price.** Such **blending** is worked from a price stand-point, and if the result is a fairly good-looking product, and if the cup is not objectionable, it is termed a fancy blend and so marketed.

To blend Coffee **properly,** various growths having **different characteristics** should be taken, and the Coffees should be used in such proportion that the result from the blend will differ from that of any of the Coffees used straight. Further than this, the beverages obtainable from a blend of this description should be preferable to the results secured from the Coffees used separately, otherwise there is **no** object in blending.

To originate a blend that is **distinctive,** that has a **pleasant aroma** and **taste,** and also one that is difficult to match, requires an **expert knowledge** of Coffee and ability to **test Coffees** in the **cup.**

Many of the so-called blends are composed principally of a good, smooth, neutral Santos, with a sufficient percentage of Bogota, Bucaramanga or Mexican Coffee to relieve the flat Santos taste. A blend of Coffee properly balanced should have a full, rich body as a basis. To this should be added one or another of the growths of Coffee having an acid character, and a further Coffee or Coffees should be used to give, if possible, an increased aroma.

A winey Bourbon Santos will be found very serviceable in many blends. Types of these Coffees have a distinct winey quality differing from other growths of Coffee, and more nearly approaching Mocha than any other type. Bourbon Coffees vary as to acidity. Some blenders will consider an extremely acid Coffee preferable, while others will prefer a Coffee showing less winey quality; but such a Coffee will add the distinct Bourbon flavor to the blend.

The winey character of certain Mexican Coffees is found to be very serviceable in high-grade blends. The flavor and aroma of the Guatemala types should not be overlooked as adding distinct characteristics to the blends in which they are used.

For the most part the backbone of the better blends of Coffee, and, in fact, many of the cheaper blends, will be one or other of the Colombian growths. Most of these Coffees are known under the general term of Bogota.

Blends of still different character are obtainable through the use of the various Coffees shipped from the Dutch East Indies, and where the consumer has been accustomed to the character given to a blend by the use of a percentage of Padang, Mandheling or Ankola Coffee, they prefer a blend of this description to the blends made up of Central and South American Coffees.

The following blends have proven very popular in their price and class:

5% Mocha
10% Maracaibo
15% Bogota
40% Santos
30% Robusta

OR

5% Mocha
10% Maracaibo
15% Bogota
15% Nicaragua
15% Robusta
40% Santos

* * * *

10% Bogota
20% Santos
20% Salvador
40% Nicaragua
10% Robusta

* * * *

30% Guatemala
30% Bogota
10% Salvador
30% Santos

* * * * *

30% Natural Robusta
40% Liberian A. J.
10% Rio
10% Costa Rica
10% Nicaragua

* * * * *

10% Mocha
20% Java
10% Bucaramanga
10% Maracaibo
20% Guatemala
30% Nicaragua

* * * *

40% Mexican
20% Bogota
20% Washed Guatemala
20% Salvador

* * * * *

10% Colombian
50% Mexican
40% Nicaragua

OR BETTER

20% Colombian
30% Guatemala
30% Nicaragua
20% Santos

20% Robusta
20% Santos
30% Salvador
30% Mexican

* * * * *

70% Rio
20% Robusta
10% Salvador

* * * *

10% Costa Rica
10% Santos
70% Robusta
10% Guatemala

* * * * *

40% Bogota
25% Santos
15% Bucaramanga
10% Mocha
10% Java

* * * * *

40% Bogota
10% Salvador
10% Nicaragua
40% Rio

* * * * *

40% Natural Nicaragua
10% Costa Rica
40% Santos
10% Salvador

* * * * *

40% Guatemala
20% Bogota
20% Salvador
20% Santos

* * * * *

50% Liberian A. J.
30% Guatemala
20% Big Bean Mexican

* * * * *

25% Mocha
75% Java

* * * * *

50% Bogota
35% Santos
15% Bucaramanga

* * * * *

60% Bogota
30% Old Brown Colombian
10% Good Bourbon Santos

70

A good point to consider in blending is to get a good, strong, smooth, sweet, heavy bodied, winey liquor; not a thin, flat, spoiled water drink. There may be better Coffees than Santos, Bogotas and Guatemalas for blending purposes, but I have never had the pleasure of meeting them. Of course, you can find a chop, once in a while, in any Coffee that is exceptionally good, but when you come to match it again you are lost, as it seems almost impossible to get two chops alike. With Bogota, Santos and Guatemala it is not so hard to match them.

One-half Guatemala, one-quarter Bogota and one-quarter Santos does not, in my opinion, make a good blend. If you make it one-half Bogota, one-quarter Guatemala and one-quarter Santos, you will have a blend that will stand up to the best of them; I know of nothing better within the price range.

COFFEE ROASTING TABLE

Sixteen Per Cent Shrinkage Including ¾c per Pound for Roasting

Green	Roasted	Green	Roasted	Green	Roasted
12	14.88	21½	26.19	31	37.50
12¼	15.18	21¾	26.48	31¼	37.79
12½	15.48	22	26.76	31½	38.09
12¾	15.78	22¼	27.08	31¾	38.39
13	16.07	22½	27.38	32	38.69
13¼	16.37	22¾	27.67	32¼	38.98
13½	16.67	23	27.97	32½	39.28
13¾	16.96	23¼	28.27	32¾	39.58
14	17.26	23½	28.57	33	39.88
14¼	17.56	23¾	28.86	33¼	40.17
14½	17.86	24	29.16	33½	40.47
14¾	18.15	24¼	29.46	33¾	40.77
15	18.45	24½	29.76	34	41.07
15¼	18.75	24¾	30.05	34¼	41.37
15½	19.05	25	30.35	34½	41.67
15¾	19.34	25¼	30.65	34¾	41.97
16	19.64	25½	30.95	35	42.26
16¼	19.94	25¾	31.25	35¼	42.56
16½	20.24	26	31.55	35½	42.86
16¾	20.54	26¼	31.85	35¾	43.15
17	20.83	26½	32.15	36	43.45
17¼	21.13	26¾	32.44	36¼	43.75
17½	21.43	27	32.74	36½	44.05
17¾	21.73	27¼	33.04	36¾	44.34
18	22.02	27½	33.34	37	44.64
18¼	22.32	27¾	33.63	37¼	44.94
18½	22.62	28	33.93	37½	45.24
18¾	22.92	28¼	34.23	37¾	45.54
19	23.21	28½	34.53	38	45.83
19¼	23.51	28¾	34.82	38¼	46.13
19½	23.81	29	35.12	38½	46.43
19¾	24.11	29¼	35.42	38¾	46.73
20	24.40	29½	35.72	39	47.02
20¼	24.70	29¾	36.01	39¼	47.32
20½	25.00	30	36.31	39½	47.62
20¾	25.30	30¼	36.61	39¾	47.92
21	25.59	30½	36.90	40	48.21
21¼	25.89	30¾	37.20		

Coffee can be made as acceptable a cool summer drink as it is the popular hot beverage of the winter. To obtain this result, the roaster must bear in mind that all cold drinks require more substance than those where heat is a factor. Coffee for icing should be so prepared as to give out a deeper colored liquor than the infusion for hot Coffee.

Those Coffees having a heavy winey or pronounced roughness, extremes in flavor, are best avoided for iced Coffee. The appeal must come first through the eye by the deeper color of the liquor; then to the palate, by the smoothness of the decoction. Bogotas of moderately winey but heavy body, well-dried high-grade Cucuta Maracaibo, combined with a soft drinking Santos, will be found as a standard to give the best results.

Careful tests demonstrate that in color of liquor, flavor and body, no moderate cost blend excels these three characters in combination. Roasted correctly, they almost defy blundering in the making, being as nearly fool-proof as can be made.

All directions for making Iced Coffee should emphasize two facts, viz: making the Coffee somewhat stronger than for hot Coffee, and that the receptacle for holding the Coffee should be placed on the Ice, not the Ice in the Coffee.

VARIOUS HIGHLY ACCEPTABLE METHODS OF BREWING COFFEES, AS, STATED BY VARIOUS AUTHORITIES

Coffee (like bread) should be cooked, not half-cooked, not over-cooked, but cooked done. This applies to both Roasting and Brewing. Care should be used in Brewing Coffee as in baking bread.

The manner of grinding or cutting the Coffee bean depends entirely upon individual taste and custom.

Coarse-ground Coffee is not generally desirable, as it requires too long an infusion to extract the full strength, and too much boiling tends to spoil both flavor and aroma.

A medium-fine grind is the most generally serviceable for ordinary home use.

There are many different formulas for preparing Coffee for the table, the majority capable of being classified under the three headings:

Infusion or Drawing: Putting the ground Coffee into boiling water and keeping it hot on the range without boiling for eight to ten minutes. With ordinary care this method will produce a very pleasing beverage, but it does not bring out much of the stimulating property of the bean.

Decoction or Boiling: Putting the ground Coffee in cold water, allowing it to come to a boil and keeping it boiling for a few seconds. This brings out more strength than the preceding method, and makes an excellent liquor, but if the boiling is continued too long, the fine aroma passes away. **A few grains of salt improves any Coffee.**

When made by boiling, a large cup of Coffee contains about 2½ grains each of tannin and caffeine, properties of the fiber or grounds which are extracted by their immersion. (**Medical authorities state that the last mentioned is a true stimulant in that it gives no reaction**). But when taken in large quantity these properties are said to affect persons of highly nervous temperament.

For the "old-fashioned" boiling method, the white of an egg is first stirred into the ground Coffee. The latter is then placed in the pot and the proper amount of boiling water is poured over it, the water, taken fresh, having previously been allowed to boil hard for ten minutes. The

Coffee is permitted to come to a good boil, is stirred thoroughly once and then placed on the back of the stove for ten minutes. If any grounds appear on top, they are stirred a little and allowed to settle. This process gives excellent results, but it requires a good deal of care.

The mistaken argument of economy is sometimes advanced in favor of boiling. Let it be known that a pound of high-grade Coffee will produce from 35 to 38 smooth, rich and delicious cups by the "drip" method, a cost of one cent per cup, the cheapest and best enjoyed article on one's table. Coffee stands as the single food product that has not doubled in price the past ten years.

Filteration or Distilling: By the use of a "percolator" the boiling water passing slowly through the ground Coffee held in the center of the machine. This method is largely used because the result is nearly always uniform. No matter which method is employed, the grounds should never be alowed to remain in the Coffee for any length of time after it is made.

In hotels, restaurants and other establishments where it is brewed in large quantities, the Coffee is generally held in a bag or other receptacle in the upper part of the urn, in order that the grounds may be more easily removed.

The best general advice to the person wishing a good cup of Coffee is to buy Coffee **as pure as possible,** and of a flavor that suits the individual taste, to have it **fresh roasted, fresh ground to moderate fineness and fresh made in a scrupulously clean Coffee-pot.**

With these points secured, a little practice will produce a fine beverage by any reasonable process. A little cold water dashed in boiling Coffee checks the boiling and causes the grounds to settle, leaving the beverage perfectly clear. In Creole cookery, the sauce result is obtained by adding a small piece of charcoal.

French Coffee: The special flavor in much of the Coffee served in France is generally due to any one or all of the three following causes: (1) the addition of 10% to 30% of Chicory, (2) the especially heavy roasting of the bean, and (3) the occasional addition of a little butter and sugar during the roasting.

It is generally made in a percolator from fine ground Coffee, the liquid being passed through percolators two or three times to acquire greater strength.

Cafe au Lait, "Coffee with Milk" or French Breakfast Coffee," generally means strong Coffee served with boiling milk, about half Coffee and half milk, or to suit the individual taste.

Cafe Noir, Black Coffee or After Dinner Coffee, requires an especially generous proportion of Coffee, and percolation continued until the liquid is black.

Demi-Tasse de Cafe, or Cafe Demitasse, means literally only a small or half-cup of Coffee, but, carelessly used, the expression has come to signify **Cafe Noir** or **After Dinner Coffee.**

Cafe a la Creme is made by adding plain or whipped cream to good **Cafe Noir. Vienna Coffee** is prepared in a special urn, which passes and re-passes the steam through the (finely ground) Coffee, thus retaining the full aroma. It is served with whipped cream.

Creole Coffee is prepared by slow percolation. The Coffee, fresh roasted and ground, is pressed compactly in the filter of the pot and a small quantity of boiling water is poured over. When this has passed through, more water is added, the process being continued at intervals of about five minutes. The result is a very strong and rich extract, which may either be served fresh or be preserved in an air-tight vessel for future use. A small quantity, even so little as a tablespoonful, of good "Creole Coffee" is sufficient for a cup of Coffee of ordinary strength.

Turkish Coffee is made from beans ground as fine as powder, placed in a pot (either large or "individual") with cold water and brought to the boiling point. It is never allowed to boil, and is served as it is without straining or settling the grounds.

Dutch Coffee is prepared by cold water process from very fine-ground Coffee held in a special filter with top and bottom reservoirs. It requires four hours or longer for the water to percolate through the Coffee, and in its passage it extracts a large percentage of strength and flavor.

Russian Coffee is strong black Coffee.

Coffee Extracts or Essence. Genuine Coffee extract is made commercially by distillation, steaming and evaporating the liquid until it is reduced to the desired strength.

One or two teaspoonfuls is generally sufficient to make a cup of Coffee of moderate strength. For household purposes, it can be made nearly the same result by following the formula for Creole Coffee.

Coffee, whether raw or roasted, should always be kept away from all strong odors, as it absorbs them very rapidly. Roasted Coffee (as already mentioned) should never be exposed to the air, as it will quickly lose its flavor and aroma.

A few things about Coffee by a Brazilian Expert:

HOW TO GRIND COFFEE

Coffee should not be ground too fine to avoid sediments and obtain it clear. The water will dissolve the essence in the coarse-ground Coffee very well. Wherever possible, Coffee should also be kept, in preference, in the bean, and ground only when needed for use. The reason is that Coffee is exceedingly susceptible to taking bad odors, especially when in the ground state. Even in the green state in the hold of a ship is liable to take bad odors from the ship, and it is well known that you can never get a good cup of Coffee on ship-board, because the ground Coffee, as soon as exposed, takes the smell and taste of salt water.

In Brazil, when the interior of a house has been freshly painted, the custom is to place a plate with ground Coffee in the middle of the room over night. Next morning the smell of fresh paint is gone from the room, but the Coffee smells and tastes like a paint-pot. It is therefore essential that all vessels used in the roasting, grinding and preparing of Coffee should be kept scrupulously clean and odorless.

HOW TO MAKE GOOD COFFEE

Coffee should never be boiled; it extracts the obnoxious compounds and gives it a disagreeable bitter taste.

Upon occasion: Mrs. Leslie Carter, the Actress, while staying at a hotel in Sedalia, Mo., complained of the abominable bitter Coffee they were serving her. The representative of a wholesale Coffee firm, who overheard her, went to the kitchen and prepared her some fresh Coffee, really good. Mrs. Carter was so pleased with it that it opened an acquaintance which resulted in Mrs. Carter engaging the salesman as her business manager.

The best way to make good Coffee is by the drip system. Numerous machines for this are on the market, all more or less on the same principle, which consists in letting hot water filter through the pulverized Coffee contained in a receptacle, the bottom of which is a fine sieve, through which the water runs off.

In the best of these machines the lower part is a receptacle containing as much water as necessary for the number of cups of Coffee required. Above this, fitting into the first, is another receptacle with a fine sieve bottom, holding the amount of ground Coffee required, ordinarily about a tablespoonful to the cup.

A metal or glass tube passes from the bottom of the lower receptacle to the top of the upper one. When the machine is put on the stove or over a lamp, the pressure of the steam developed forces the boiling water through the tube to the upper receptacle, when it spreads out over the Coffee, filters through it and runs through the sieve to the bottom. This continues until the Coffee has the desired strength.

A good way, too, and much used in Brazil and Europe, is the "old-fashioned" way of putting ground Coffee into a conical sack of clean new linen, held open by a wire ring, and hanging it over a can. Hot water is then poured over the Coffee and repoured, until it is strong enough. Before using it, the sack should be boiled in Coffee to extract the odor and taste of the new linen.

In all cases the greatest care should be taken that all utensils are always kept scrupulously clean. If the Coffee is made in metal machines, it should be transferred to a porcelain jug as soon as it is made, and the machine carefully cleaned, as Coffee attacks all metals, especially copper.

It is also essential that the water used in making Coffee be pure and clear, and contain no mineral salts. It should not be boiling, but of a temperature that you can just put your finger in without scalding. Boiling water not only volatilizes the aromatic essences, but extracts the obnoxious compounds which give the Coffee a disagreeable taste.

Connoisseurs who are very particular about this beverage go so far as to use only cold water in extracting their Coffee. They have the patience to put it in a porcelain filter, pour cold water on it over and over again until it is strong enough.

Then they put the can containing the infusion into a hot water bath; that is, another vessel containing boiling water, and heat it to the boiling point.

Others, again, put the ground Coffee in a covered porcelain pot with sufficient cold water and let it stand for ten to twelve hours. Then they carefully pour off the liquid, or filter it, and heat it in a hot water bath. This certainly is the way to obtain the most delicious Coffee, because it retains all the aroma and fine flavor without dissolving any of the obnoxious bitter-tasting components.

Coffee should be drunk as soon as possible after making it, and not kept standing too long. Nor should it be kept over and warmed up again, as it loses its flavor by standing.

COFFEE DRINKING IN BRAZIL

In Brazil, where you get the most delicious Coffee in the world, and Coffee making has developed into an art, there is a saying that Coffee, to be good, should be: "Black as Night, Hot as Hell and Sweet as Love."

In fact, however, a real good cup of Coffee, as you get it in the leading Cafes in Rio or Sao Paulo, is not black as night or so very strong, but of a chestnut color, so clear and transparent that you can almost see the bottom of the cup and it leaves an amber stain.

It should froth like chocolate, and its fragrant aroma should fill the room. There are no saloons or bars in Brazil, and Coffee takes the place of "Social" drink, of high-ball or cocktail.

There are Cafes in every street that make a specialty of serving only Coffee. Their wide open doors, little round marble-topped tables, with small cups and saucers set up around a sugar basin, make inviting pictures.

You sit down, pull a cup towards you, and immediately an attendant comes and fills it with delicious hot Coffee, for which you lay down a nickel coin of 100 Reis, equal to three cents.

If you pay a social visit, or call on the President of the Republic, or any high official, the first thing you will observe is a servant coming in with a tray of cups and saucers and a Coffee-can, to hand you a cup of fragrant hot Coffee. After you have taken that you proceed to state your business.

Americans may laugh at this and call it unbusiness-like, but it cannot be denied that this show of hospitality will remove any restraint and put you at your ease, while the stimulating effect of the hot Coffee clears your ideas.

In this way the average Brazilian business man, or politician, or whatever he may be, takes on an average in a day from one to two dozen small cups of black Coffee, and he not only survives it, but keeps healthy, works quite as hard as the average American business man, and maintains a clearer brain and steadier nerves than if he had fortified himself with a dozen high-balls. And this in spite of what "Postum" and other speculative competitors(?) have to say concerning the injurious effects of Coffee.

To this habit of continually taking small cups of black Coffee during the day may be ascribed to the limitation of the use of alcoholic drinks and the absence of inebriate persons in Brazil, for Coffee seems to create an aversion to them in the system.

The Brazilian is accustomed to take a light wine with his meals, but never an alcoholic drink between meals, especially no spirits

One (considered good) authority says: **Avoid cream with Coffee.**

Coffee taken with hot milk in the morning, or, in fact, any time, is an excellent aliment, a meal in itself, we may say. Beware, however, of taking Coffee with a lot of cream in it, together with your meals, as is generally the custom throughout the United States

The fat in the cream enters with certain components in the Coffee into a combination which is not only indigestible in itself, but obstructs the digestion of the accompanying meals and other rich foods, and will lead in time to chronic indigestion and stomach, heart and liver troubles.

And if "Postum" and other competitors (?) bring forward as an argument, cases of where the continued use of Coffee has become in time injurious to the system, it has been owing to the fact that the persons in question have been in the habit of using badly prepared Coffee with a lot of rich cream as the customary drink with their meals.

On the other hand, a small cup of well-prepared, good, hot, black Coffee taken a short time after your meals, will cause a pleasant well-feeling and contentment, because, taken in that way, it increases the secretion of gastric juice, and has a marvelous effect upon the digestion.

HOW TO PREPARE THE BEVERAGE FOR HOTELS, CAFES AND RESTAURANTS

Making Coffee in a Coffee Urn for Hotels or Restaurants is decidedly the practical way to make Coffee in an Urn. Coffee that will' please your trade, requires first a clean textile bag suspended about two-thirds of the way to the bottom. Percolating quietly through the bag and repouring is the only process known giving the best results.

Never use Urns that blow steam through the Coffee. They may use less Coffee, but the resulting liquor is not clear, neither is it aromatic. Filter Paper strainers are frail, and do not allow the Coffee to seep through, so it is best to avoid the method that employs them.

HOW COFFE SHOULD BE ROASTED AND GROUND

The Coffee should be roasted to a dark chestnut color. When roasted **too** high, the beverage becomes bitter; when **too low**, it tastes raw.

Grind the Coffee so as to resemble granulated sugar. **Coarse** ground Coffee gives little strength, too **finely** ground retards filtering and frequently leaves a brackish taste. Watch your Coffee mill closely, adjust and oil it occasionally; nearly all mills work loose.

Use from 10 to 12 ounces of Coffee **to each gallon** of water for regular Coffee, and from 12 to 16 ounces of Coffee to **each gallon** of water for after-dinner Coffee.

More or less Coffee may be used, should these amounts not suit the demand of your trade.

First wet or moisten the bag inside the Urn, then pour the Coffee in the bag; pour through it bubbling boiling water, use no other. Simply because water vaporizing or steaming does not always mean that it is at the boiling point, and unless it is at the bubbling boiling point, it will not mix with the oil of the Coffee.

This is one of the most important essentials in brewing good Coffee.

Next re-pour the liquid Coffee through the grounds until all the liquid has been through the ground Coffee at least twise. Let this stand four or five minutes, it is then ready to serve if required. Nothing is needed to settle it. It will be perfectly clear but not so strong as later. The bag containing the grounds should remain in the Urn 30 to 40 minutes, but no longer.

The desired strength will be extracted without any bitterness whatever, if these instructions are followed. The seeping through of the liquid gives the Coffee that desirable cooked taste.

THE CARE OF BAGS AND URNS IMPORTANT

Wash your bags thoroughly in hot water, but use no soap. (A small pinch of soda will help.) Rinse in cold water and let them remain in cold water until needed. Dry bags absorb every odor of the kitchen. Always have two bags for each urn in use, and start new ones every Sunday or at any rate once a week.

Wash the urns every night with soda or powder and hot water. Rinse them with hot water, then with cold water. While so doing leave the faucet open and the lid off of the urn, so that the air may circulate freely.

Always serve cream with your Coffee if possible. Always let your customer (or guest) be the judge as to how much or how little. He unquestionably knows his individual taste and requirements better than you. At most, little is needed, and the **Coffee** is so much better without it. Have your cups warm and your pots very, very hot. China pots are the best to be used.

By taking pains and following the directions as above given, your Coffee thus obtained will help materially to make your breakfast trade grow. It is the Coffee, Rolls and Butter that make it successful.

COFFEE BLENDS FOR RESTAURANTS

William B. Harris, the Government's Coffee expert, believes that the Coffee of prime importance in preparing restaurant blends is **Bogota.** He advises the use of a full-bodied **Bogota** and a **winey, Bourbon Santos** in the proportion of 75% **Bogota** and 25% **Santos.**

Blends may also be made up from combinations of **Bogota, Mexicans** and **Guatemalas.**

According to Mr. Harris, the average blend of good Coffee when made up 2½ pounds to 5 gallons of water, will produce a liquor of good color and strength. For many hotels, however, this may not answer, as it is not heavy enough.

No steward, hotel or restaurant man should ever advertise Coffee on his menu, and then serve a drink employing Chicory (or any other substitute), because, while there is no Federal law against such a practice, there are State laws against it, and every customer would gladly subscribe to a Moral law which would make it misbranding.

Hotel men should purchase their Coffee in the bean and do their own grinding. Then they need never have cause to complain that their Coffee man deceived them, or that some salesman misled them.

The hotel steward wishing to serve his patrons with a good heavy-bodied Coffee, particularly a black after-dinner Coffee, should use three, four, or even four and a half pounds of ground Coffee to five gallons of water.

WAYS SUGGESTED FOR SERVING COFFEE. HONEY, FOR INSTANCE

Perhaps you have never flavored your Coffee with honey. Yet you can search a long time before you can taste anything more delicious than a perfect cup of Coffee sweetened with some perfect sweet clover honey. Of course, you would not use honey in the comb. Strained honey, or better still, the newer solidified, or granulated, honey gives the best results.

The Coffee may be served either black or topped with whipped cream. Probably, served in this way, the Coffee is best suited to after lunch, or after tea, service; without the cream, it may take the place of the familiar Cafe Noir.

There is no better luncheon accompaniment to the honeyed Coffee than some delicious, old-fashioned sponge or nut cake.

For afternoon tea, try it with cinnamon toast, and after dinner use it alone with its delicious self.

MARSHMALLOWS, A DAINTY SWEETENING

Speaking of the after-dinner Coffee, or Coffee particularly suited to party service, are you familiar with Marshmallows as sweetening agent? No! Well, just drop two in a medium-sized cup, then fill it with Coffee. The result will be a delightful sweetness, with a frothy foam on the top which somewhat resembles cream. If you like, you can add a little plain cream also to the beverage, but it is not necessary.

When serving this at dinner, you will find it delicious when accompanied by some simple cake or wafers, flavored with vanilla and containing either cocoanut or nuts.

The same combination would be suitable for a party, or a little French pastry could be used if desired. If the Coffee is served from the pantry, a dessert spoonful of Marshmallow Creme to the medium-sized cup may be used instead of the Marshmallow proper.

One of the reasons why Marshmallows are so well adapted to Coffee is because of the vanilla flavoring which they contain. Sometimes a drop or two of this extract may be served in each cup of Coffee, or the Coffee may be topped with sweetened whipped cream flavored with vanilla, as is done so much in foreign countries.

In this case, the Coffee should be served as a part of the dessert, because the whipped cream is so rich.

A harmonious accompaniment to this consists of fruit tarts, such as strawberry, raspberry, or little orange pies, or a cake or cooky which is rather highly seasoned with spice.

"COFFEE MARASCHINO" (Bone-dry)

Now that the old type of Coffee, with brown sugar and brandy, is no longer being served, "Coffee Maraschino" will undoubtedly take its place,

86

especially as Maraschino Cherries are now being put up without liquor.

In this case, a demitasse is used, the Coffee being flavored with a little of the liquid from the Maraschino Cherries and a cherry or two being dropped into each cup.

Cream, either plain or whipped, may be used or not, as desired. If served as "black Coffee' at the end of a dinner, there should be no accompaniment, unless, perhaps, that of the usual bon-bons, but if served as part of the dessert course at luncheon, almost any kind of cake is a suitable accompaniment, except one containing chocolate.

But in any case, when making the Coffee, be sure to put in a few grains of salt.

SALT TO "MELLOW" COFFEE

Have you ever tried adding a few grains of salt to your cup of Coffee? You will be surprised to find how the flavor is improved. It attains an indescribable mellowness.

Of course, there is a reason, and in this case it is the addition of just the right amount of alkali to neutralize the slight acidity of the Coffee (It also overcomes the more or less raw taste produced by the woody fibre of the Coffee) for all occasions, and it is absolutely essential when Coffee is used as the flavoring agent of various desserts, otherwise the taste is "empty."

MAPLE SUGAR

Again, have you ever tried Maple Sugar as a Coffee sweetener? You may have heard of it during the sugar shortage of the war, and afraid, perhaps, that it would not taste good, and clung tenaciously to your white sugar. In reality, it is delicious, for there is something about the flavors of Maple and Coffee that harmonize.

That is one reason why a cup of Coffee and a plate of griddle cakes or waffles with Maple Syrup is a perfect combination.

As to the amount of Maple Sugar to use in sweetening the Coffee, just serve it in the sugar bowl, broken into little lumps, and appetite will do the rest.

FONDANT

Brown Sugar, flavored with strong Coffee and cooked with a pinch of cream of tartar, makes a delicious fondant, which every home candy-maker should know about during the white sugar shortage.

COFFEE FONDANT

Three-quarters cupful very strong, hot Coffee, 2½ cupfuls brown sugar, ⅛ teaspoonful cream of tartar.

Combine the three ingredients in a very smooth, clean saucepan and stir over a slow heat until they are dissolved; heat gradually to boiling point, and boil without stirring until, when tried in cold water, a little of the mixture will keep its shape in the form of a soft ball. With a candy thermometer the temperature will be 238° F. Pour the fondant onto a slightly buttered, large platter; let it stand for a few minutes to cool, until, when pressed with finger, a dent is left on the surface and yet there is no crust. When this occurs, scrape the fondant together and work it with a wooden spoon, or smooth stick, until it is creamy in color and texture. When it becomes creamy, begin to knead it, and knead it until it is formed into a smooth ball. Put it into a bowl, cover it with a damp cloth and let it stand a day before using.

If desired, this fondant may be flavored in different ways, and the best time to add the flavoring is just before it is kneaded. A few drops of vanilla may be put in one portion, a drop each of clove and cinnamon extract in another portion, and a little maple flavoring in another. The fondant is then ready to use in any way desired.

WAYS TO USE COFFEE FONDANT

Shape the fondant into small, round balls; let them stand a few hours in a cool place, and then dip them in chocolate. To do this, cut the chocolate in small pieces, using preferably confectioners' dipping chocolate, which may be purchased at a caterer's. Put it in a double boiler, let it stand over hot water until melted, then beat it frequently until cooled, and it is of the consistency of molasses. Dip in the centers, with a hat pin; let them drain a moment, and then transfer them to oiled paper, to become firm.

COFFEE FONDANT SLICES

، Flavor one-half the recipe for Coffee Fondant with Vanilla, and work it into a roll about as wide in diameter as a half dollar. Let this stand a few hours, dip it in chocolate, roll in finely-chopped walnuts, and when firm, cut it with a sharp knife in slices a fourth-inch thick.

COFFEE BON-BONS

Shape the centers as directed in Ways to Use Coffee Fondant, and dip them, after standing a few hours, in plain or Raspberry Fondant, melted to the consistency of very thick cream.

COFFEE MAPLE CHOCOLATES

Combine equal parts of Coffee Fondant with soft, grated maple sugar. Shape into small balls and dip into chocolate, as previously directed, or merely roll in finely-chopped, toasted almonds or Brazil nuts.

QUICK COFFEE FONDANT

One tablespoonful butter, 2 tablespoonfuls very strong Coffee, 1 tablespoonful cream or undiluted evaporated milk, 1-3 teaspoonful vanilla extract, soft brown sugar to knead (from 2½ to 3 cupfuls).

Cream the butter in a rather deep, medium-sized bowl, and with a wooden spoon work in a little of the sugar. Then gradually add the Coffee and evaporated milk, mixed with the vanilla, alternately with sufficient sugar to make the mixture stiff enough to knead. Knead well, cover with a damp cloth and let stand for a little while. Then use in any recipe calling for Coffee Fondant.

COFFEE MARSHMALLOW FUDGE

One-half cupful very strong Coffee, 2 cupfuls light-brown sugar, 1-3 tablespoonful butter or good margarine, ½ teaspoonful vanilla, ⅛ teaspoonful cream of tartar, a few grains of salt, ¾ cupful fresh marshmallows cut in quarters.

Combine the sugar, cream of tartar, salt, butter and coffee in a medium-sized saucepan and cook without stirring over moderate heat until a soft ball is formed when a little is tried in cold water. A candy thermometer will register 238° F. Cool slightly but do not let a crust form. Then add the marshmallows and vanilla, beat until creamy and pour into a buttered pan to cool, making a mixture about a half-inch deep. Before it is entirely cold cut it into squares. Chopped nut-meats may be substituted for the marshmallows if desired.

COFFEE COCOANUT PRALINES

Observe the proportions and directions for making Coffee Marshmallow Fudge, but omit the marshmallows. Just before removing the mixture from the heat, add a cupful of shredded cocoanut. When tepid, beat the mixture until creamy and drop it by tablespoonfuls onto oiled paper, for Pralines are always large.

COFFEE NUT PRALINES

Make according to the directions for Coffee Cocoanut Pralines, substituting a cupful of chopped walnut meats for the cocoanut

CREAM COFFEE DROPS

One-half cupful very strong Coffee, 2 cupfuls light-brown sugar, ⅛ teaspoonful cream of tartar, a choice of vanilla, cinnamon and clove, or maple flavoring.

Combine all the ingredients, except the flavoring, in a medium-sized saucepan; stir over a slow heat until dissolved, then do not stir any further, but cook until a soft ball is formed when a little of the mixture is tried in cold water—that is, 238° F. by the candy thermometer. Cool until lukewarm, flavor, beat until creamy, transfer to a small pitcher and drop onto oiled paper, in amounts large enough to form candies of the shape of an ordinary cream peppermint.

COFFEE CHOCOLATE CARAMELS

One-third cupful very strong Coffee, 1-3 cupful rich milk, 2-3 cupful molasses, 3 cupfuls brown sugar, 3 squares (oz.) chocolate, 7 tablespoonfuls butter, or half butter and half very good margarine, ½ teaspoonful vanilla, 1 cupful coarsely-chopped walnut or hickory nut-meats, pecans or toasted, chopped Brazil nuts.

Combine all the ingredients, except the nut-meats and vanilla, and boil them slowly until, when a little is tried in cold water, a ball of caramel texture is formed, 248° F. by the candy thermometer. Flavor, stir in the nuts, beat a moment, then pour into a good-sized bread pan, which has been lined with wax paper. The mixture should be an inch deep. When half cold, cut in squares. Then transfer in the sheet to a bread board, cut and wrap each one separately in waxed paper before packing.

EARLY HISTORY AND MYTHICAL LEGENDS OF THE TEA PLANT

The first discovery of the virtue of the beverage obtained by the infusion of Tea-leaves in water, is hidden in the obscurity of ancient history.

One Chinese tradition gives the credit to some Buddhist priests, who, unable to use the brackish water near their temple, steeped in it the leaves of a shrub growing in the vicinity, with the intention of correcting the unpleasant properties. The experiment was so successful that they spread the news among their neighbors and subsequently engaged in the extensive cultivation of the plant.

Another Legend of the Origin of Tea. The Chinese have a legend purporting to account for the origin of **Tea** in China. Owing to the dense population and poor sanitation, frequent epidemics of typhoid and other fevers were prevalent and nearly wiped out at times large sections of the population. The wise men of the empire were called together to suggest a remedy. They found that the drinking waters were polluted, but by boiling these waters before drinking practically all danger was removed. An edict went forth that, throughout the kingdom, the people should boil their water before drinking. By strict obedience to this law the epidemic and fevers ceased. But the people grew careless, the law was violated, more and more, and again the disorders appeared. The wise men were again called to overcome the difficulty. They were sent in search of an herb whose delicious flavors could only be brought out by boiling water, and the search resulted in the discovery of the now famous **Tea** plant.

As mythology plays its part in the earliest records of Tea, the fable in this case is credited to a Dutch traveler named **Koempfer,** who relates how a **Buddhist** monk came to **China** from **India** sometime during the fifth century of the Christian era, and, vexed at having slumbered during a night of vigil and prayer, **cut off** his eyelids, casting them on the ground, whence immediately sprang up two **Tea plants.**

This legend has often been repeated in popular works, as not only prefiguring the anti-somnolent properties of the leaf, but as affording readditional evidence of the source and probable period of introduction of the Tea plant into the **Flowery Kingdom.**

In China, however, this legend seems altogether unknown, while the plant itself has been known there from remote ages.

Another record attributes its discovery, about 2737 B. C., to Chin Nung, a celebrated scholar and philosopher, to whom nearly all agricultural and medical knowledge is traced in **China.**

In replenishing a fire made of the branches of the **Tea plant,** some of the leaves fell into the vessel in which he was boiling water for his evening meal. The consumption of the beverage thus formed, the first **"Pot of Tea",** proved so exhilirating in effect that he formed the habit of so using the leaves. Later he imparted to others the knowledge thus accidentally gained, and in a short time it became the common property of the Empire.

China is quite generally acknowledged as the birth place of the Tea industry. Some writers reason that the honor belongs to India or Japan, but other authorities name the thirteenth century as seeing the first use of Tea in the latter country.

Dr. Bretschneider is credited with having discovered the earliest recorded mention of Tea in literature, who, towards the latter end of the last century was physician to the Russian legation at Pekin.

The doctor probed deeply into ancient Chinese literature, and discovered a reference to Tea in a Chinese compilation known as the **Pent Sao,** 2700 B. C., while in a work dated 400 A. D. a full description of the plant and the present modes of

infusion were found. Its antiquity in **China** is ·
practically undoubted, and the probability is that
its introduction into **Japan** took place at a later
period, but we can only surmise as to that.

What is known, however, is that the Tea plant
was found in 1824 or thereabouts, growing wild in
the forests of **Assam,** apparently in an indigenous
state. These forests clothe the hills which form
the boundary between **India** and **China,** and it is
fair assumption that the plant or its seed was
thousands of years ago exported from India into
China, where it became an important industry.

Tea was brought to **Europe** in the Sixteenth
Century, the **Dutch East India Company** intro-
ducing it into **Holland.**

The first authenticated mention of it in England
is in the year 1657, at which time it was considered
a very rare luxury. It was known as early as
1680 in the **American Colonies,** selling at from **five**
to **six dollars a pound** for the **cheapest** varieties.

Its use was for many years widely condemned
by writers and preachers, who attributed to it numerous qualities inimical to health, morals and the
public order, but that attitude was long ago rele-
gated to oblivion, and the enormous quantity now
consumed places it among the most important of
food articles.

· Its title comes from **"Te",** the Chinese name for
Tea in **Amoy** dialect. In other parts of China it is
known as Ta, Cha, Dzo, etc.

In its wild state the Tea plant is a small evergreen tree, of which there are several varieties,
and similar in appearance to the Camellia, to
which it is botanically related. The Assam type
in its wild state grows to a height of fifteen to
thirty feet, with numerous branches and a wealth
of lance-like leaves, which often attain a length of
six to nine inches.

The China varieties and the numerous crosses
are more dwarf in habit and of smaller leaf. The

rather large, white, fragrant flowers grow singly, or two together, in the axils of the leaves.

. Under cultivation, the shrubs are not allowed to exceed three to five feet in height, and flowering is permitted only for seed purposes.

If the Tea bush was not continually plucked over, for its leaves, it would grow into a tall, willowy tree. The bushes are frequently allowed to grow in this way (without plucking), as seed-bearing plants, and it is from the unplucked trees that the seed is gathered. The flowers first appear, then the pod containing the seeds, which are three small nuts like filberts, and have an oily, bitter taste, and usually ripen in October.

Before planting, the seed is tested to find out its germinating qualities, and then placed in seed beds, which are carefully shaded from the fierce heat of the Sun, until the young plant is old enough to be transplanted into the field, garden, or plantation. At this time the plant is usually ten to twelve inches high, and when it is about four years old it bears its first crop, locality, soil, etc,. being the determining factor to some extent, but a year or more before the crop is expected, it is cut down to a foot or less. It is again cut down to about two feet three months before gathering, the object being to make the bush spread and to stimulate the fullest possible growth of the "flushes" or young shoots which furnish the tender, succulent new leaves desired.

After this operation, it is plucked regularly for eighteen months to two years, the bushes yielding new "flushes" at frequent intervals, when it is again pruned back to allow it to rest.

. With proper care and under favoroble conditions its bearing life is practically unlimited.

The whole process of cultivation is to insure regular, frequent and vigorous "flushing". From the upper part or flat surface of the bush there continually sprout out long, green, tender shoots bearing young leaves. The bud at the tip, and one, two or three leaves below it are nipped off by the skillful fingers of a coolie woman or child. (The plucking is usually delegated to women and children.)

When the bud and one leaf is taken, the plucking is termed "fine"; when two leaves are taken, "medium", and when three, "coarse"

Medium plucking is generally practiced. The foregoing system of plucking applies particularly to Indian, Ceylon and Java Teas, and is practically applicable to all other Tea plants. Only the shoots mentioned above are gathered as a rule, and care is taken to avoid damaging the leaf-bud in the axil below the leaves taken, as that in its turn soon develops into a new "flush". Of course, the whole "flush" may be taken or only the choicer upper part, according both to the size of the shoot and the minimum grade leaf desired.

The rapidity and accuracy of the experienced "picker" is almost incredible.

The young leaves of all varieties are very similar in general appearance when fresh plucked. The larger leaves differ considerably in general proportions, but they always retain the characteristic construction which renders it easy to detect the addition of leaves from other plants.

The quality of the Tea leaf before preparation depends on: (1) The locality (even the poorest product of an upland garden is often choicer than the best low-lying garden); (2) soil composition (minerals contained for this play an important part in determining flavor); (3) selection of the leaves (by including some of the older leaves the crop may be greatly increased, but the grade is correspondingly lowered); and (4) the judgment exercised in the time of plucking.

The weather also exerts a great influence. When the rain falls equably and a bright sun appears after heavy showers, the plants become rich with new shoots, and the leaves bright green, elastic in texture and rich in flavor.

When too much rain falls at one time, shoots and leaves became hardened and less flexible. If there is too little moisture, they become stunted and sapless.

In Ceylon, where there is no Winter, the picking takes place every eight to ten days all the year round, but in China and Japan there are four principal harvest periods.

The earliest buddings, pale-green and very delicate, are gathered in the beginning of April, and are termed "first-picking. In China, these, as a rule, realize high prices and are consumed chiefly by the wealthy classes in China and Russia, very little reaching other markets.

The first general gathering commences in May, and it is from this collection that we receive the finest China Tea of commerce, known to the trade as "first crop tea". Then follows the later picking, known as "second crop tea", and again a third and fourth, the crop gradually becoming lower in quality as the season proceeds, a large percentage of the late harvests being consumed locally and made into "Brick Tea".

All kinds of Tea comes from the same shrubs, the main difference between "Green" and "Black" being that Black Tea is fermented and Green Tea is not. The number of varieties of prepared Tea, both Green and Black, is due to the sorting of the leaves into different sizes, and to local difference in making and blending.

Prior to the sorting, the freshly-picked shoots undergo four main processes, if Black Tea is required: withering, rolling, fermenting and firing. For green Tea, fermenting is omitted.

The shoots for Black Tea are first spread on shelves of wire or jute-hessian to "wither", the object being to allow the sap and other moisture to evaporate until the leaf is soft and flaccid for "twisting" in the rollers. The shelves are very loosely woven, so that the air can pass through them freely.

The time required for this process varies widely, sometimes twenty-four hours, occasionally much longer. If the weather is damp, artificial heat is generally employed.

For Green Tea, in order to avoid fermentation, steaming for a short time is substituted for the withering process.

The withering shoots are put through rollers, which squeeze out any excess moisture and give the "twist" which results in the characteristic form of the prepared leaf. The appearance of the leaf or "roll", as it is technically termed, when taken out of the roller, is a mess of mashy lumps. This is put through a roll-breaker, which breaks up the lumps and sifts the detached leaves and young stems through the wire mesh into cloths placed below to receive them.

For the Green Tea, the product from the roll-breaker immediately undergoes "firing"

For Black Tea, it is spread out in wooden frames, covered with wet clothes and allowed to ferment until the leaves attain a bright copper tint, the color which they should have in the tea-pot after infusion. The extent to which fermentation is permitted is determined by the smell and appearance of the leaf, points that require experienced judgment, as too little means rawness and bitterness, and any excess destroys much or all of the flavor.

For "firing" the Tea is spread thinly upon wire trays and placed in the siracco or desiccator, where a current of hot air, from 190° to 240° F. passes through it. It emerges thoroughly dry and brittle, the finished Tea, requiring only sorting and packing to be ready for market. About 4200 pounds of green shoots are required to make 1,000 pounds of the prepared article.

After cooling over night, the Tea goes to the sifter, a machine with a series of sloping sieves, one above the other.

The sieves are shaken by engine or motor power,

at a very high speed, and the tea falls through from one sieve to another, each sieve retaining a different size, and emptying itself into a chest through a spout at the low end.

The leaves and stems retained by the top sieve: i e., the largest, form the "ordinary" grades of Tea. Each size smaller is correspondingly choicer, excepting the last, known as "dust" or "dust and siftings" or "fannings", sold at low prices.

The second sieve retains (in Black Tea) **Pekoe** or **Pekoe Souchong**, according to the crop or the estate policy; the third, **Pekoe** or **Orange Pekoe**; and the fourth, **Orange Pekoe** or **Broken Orange Pekoe**, or "Flowery Pekoe" (so called because of its cup quality).

The term "**Pekoe**" refers to the downy appearance of the undersides and ends of the young leaves, and "**Orange**" to the color of the ends of the still newer leaves and to the "tips" or leaf-buds, which look like little chips of wood and are also commercially classed as "**Golden Tips**".

The **tips** give the tea a good appearance and add greatly to its strength and flavor. They are sometimes separated and offered as **Pure Golden Tips**, selling in **London** for as high as fifty **dollars** a pound.

When the **sorting** is done largely **by hand**, as in China and Japan, the size grades are much more numerous.

Caper is a **Black Tea** very much resembling the green **Gunpowder** in shape.

In the **Green Teas**, the sorting produces the different sizes of **Gunpowder, Young Hyson,** etc. (See China Green Teas.)

Uncolored Green Tea varies in tint from yellow to greenish brown. The grey-green of the **China** and **Japan** Teas imported prior to May 1, 1911, was due to the addition of a minute quantity of coloring powder during the firing.

The various grades, after a frequent supplementary picking over by hand, are day by day, stored away in their separate bins, until there is enough to make what is known technically, as a "break", 5,000 pounds and upwards.

The next operation is bulking. The whole contents of the bins of one grade are thrown together and agitated by scoops or shovels until so thoroughly, mixed that each pound of Tea will be the same as another in flavor and appearance. Finally comes the packing in chests, cans and packages, the Tea in the first two cases being shaken down to make it lay close. The numerous processes of preparation are responsible for the broken condition of most of the leaves in the product finally marketed.

Most of the Tea dust which accumulates in manufacture and as the result of transportation and commercial handling, is of very fine quality. If protected from contamination, and properly cared for in other respects, it makes good liquor.

There is strong prejudice against its use in America, partly, perhaps, because it lends itself so readily to adulterations, but in England it commands a ready sale, as, used in the correct proportions, it improves the blend, adding to its strength and pungency. In Tea-growing countries it is a common practice to pulverize the leaves by rubbing in the hand, dropping the powder into the drinking cups in which it is steeped.

The foregoing description gives a general idea of the method now employed in making India and Ceylon Teas, both Black and Green, but the principles used are those also used in the preparation of China and Japan Teas, the chief difference being that in the two latter countries machinery plays a comparatively unimportant part. Much of the firing is done in pots, bowls or baskets over charcoal fires, and the twisting by placing the leaves in bags and rolling them with the hands.

In China there is a strong contrast between the busy season and the slack time which follows it.

In an interesting article, published prior to the recent introduction of modern methods, the Foo-chow Herald said: "A Tea -packing house at this season presents a very different scene from that of two months before. Then one found long lines of catty boxes waiting to be soldered up. Now none. Next, one found fat bags stacked up eight or ten feet high, bursting with Tea that escaped here and there through holes temporarily stopped with bamboo leaves; the bottom of the bags mostly stained from contact with wet flights of mountain stairs upon which the exhausted coolies had set them down on the passage. Now one finds but empty chests, hundreds in number."

"Farther on, one came to the dozen long rows of sifters facing each other, forty in a row, the mesh of some taking a pencil, that of others re-fusing a pencil point, sifting Tea leaf, rough and bold, that, after a persuasive grasp or two of the hand, broke and consented, after a few shakes of the sieve, to be stripped of some of the sappy leaf-edges and leaf-ends, and to appear below, the even and uniform leaf which the Tea-drinker in-sists he must have (plus the dust due to the per-suading). The transformation in a rough leaf in passing through the meshes of a coarse sieve, with a gentle crush from the sifter's hand, en-hances a rough, bold Tea very considerably in value."

"In place of the rows of men then seen tilting and jerking their sieves in a monotony only broken by the contonese taskmaster's roll-call twice a day before the general meal of fish and rice, there is now to be seen only the bare floor of hardened earth, piles of empty benches stacked in a corner and the sieves of the twelve different sizes used, each in its division in the three-story stands."

"The dozen or score of fanning mills are still, too. The Tea-leaf separated in these fanning mills has been sold, and the mills will rest until another

May shall bring courage back to the pale and dispirited native teamen."

"There are stacked in this huge go-down, a few hundred packages of the native maker's brick Tea wrapped in plaited bamboo strips, bound in half bamboo and triply rattaned. Aside here, its manufacture still continues. The Chinese upper millstone is being turned upon the nether by a Chinaman who is grinding Tea seeds left by a fanning mill, and in these sycee-boxes sharp spades are falling upon the stems, chopping them fine enough to go into the stemmy, dusty mixture to which the seed dust gives the strength, while the chopped stems vouch for its being Tea."

"In the firing house are the four Chinese rice kettles, two feet across the mouth, which, when in use, set obliquely upon edge, turn the Tea back in a shower over the hand of the stirrer, a wood fire being kept up in the brick work underneath."

"Fire holes also, scores in number, follow in rows the walls of the firing house, in each an iron charcoal pan. Over each of these fires is a huge hourglass-shaped basket-hood or muffler that shuts in all the heat of each fire to but one outlet, that through the Tea sieve which chokes the throat of each basket. In these baskets is dried the Tea that comes in from the hills, wet or flat from constant downpour and from the first fermentation of the leaf."

"Here, too, on the floor above, the benches are empty, the benches where girls and women came to sort the rough stems from the leaf, getting half a cent for removing them from the two catties of Tea apportioned to them, in wound bamboo-woven trays."

"The floor is now bare where we then saw the ninghteh Tea brought to a uniform shade, by shaking the bags with a few spoonfuls of lamp black, then bulked upon the floor, to be strewn white as a spring grave with the pure Muhli blossoms; the blossoms in turn burried under another avalanche of funeral Tea, and this again with blossoms, life upon death, then both rudely mingled together and put away in boxes for a night till the fragrance had been robbed by the dead Tea, the faded flowers being finally thrown aside, spent and worthless."

"Our round finished at the shed, where, out of long sheets of lead, Chinese lads were glibly making lead cases by molding them, hatter like, upon a box, and then running the soldering iron along the edges. Other Chinamen, in their natal costume, were washing off the dust and sweat of the day at a huge four-hogshead vat of hot water. There, too, were piles of wood for the hot tea coppers, crates of up river hardwood charcoal for the firing pans and the firing baskets."

"We must leave without the sight we then had of the mad dervish dance of two Chinese, who given a dozen pounds of tea stems in a tray under their sandals perform about the interior periphery of a double shuffle, twist and grind that is cooler for the spectator, the thermometer in the nineties, than for the performers from whose bodies the perspiration rolls into the tea stems below."

"The box factory is elsewhere. We enter on our homeward way. It is in another old disused tea hong, occupied by foreigners in the days when money was made, tumbled down now and abandoned to Chinese. Inside a few Chinese youths, eating a dollar's worth of rice per month, were rapidly gluing and dove-tailing together, by rough wholesale strokes, boxes by the score. Few nails are used, for these are hand-made and cannot be afforded. What a bungling "mending" the merchant pays for when these frail cases reach the land of rough usage and coarse nails."

"There you saw a bit of thin teakwood; there a bit of paper gaudily daubed with cardinal colors, a stroke or two, side marries end, the gaudy paper cover hides all joints, and the catty boxes, gay

104

with bird, butterfly, dragon and phoenix, are **en route** to be stared at in a far off grocer's window."

"Every season sees vast quantities of tea pass through the sieves in hundreds of packing houses, some in hamlets in the hills, some, as in **Foochow,** in cities ten to fifty miles from the hills, much of it brought in by women who have carried it up and down the mountain pathways, twenty-five miles a day, regardless of their bent backs, their only food often a double handful of salt to bite before they drink."

"Probably all tea leaving **Foochow** has been lifted up and down as much as if it had been carried up one side of the great pyramid and down the other a score of times. Boatmen at river marts have fought pitched battles for it, their livelihood depending upon its transport, and plenty of their men have been ready to fight for the privilege of carrying it, women, also under their loads, behind their husbands."

The foregoing picture relates to tea making in 1874. Modern methods have already been described.

CONSUMPTION AND PRINCIPAL VARIETIES

The consumption of **Green Tea,** twenty or thirty years ago the standard variety, has to a considerable extent given place to the taste for **Black Tea.**

An equally important commercial change has been the increase in favor of **Ceylon** and **India Teas,** (also the better grades of **Java Teas**) at the expense of the **China** and **Japanese** varieties. Imports from the two last named countries have been greatly reduced during the last few years.

When to this loss of trade from the United States is coupled a still greater diminution in the English market, where **Ceylon** and **India Teas,** particularly, are most popular. For after China and Japan, (and Australia) England is the world's largest per-capita Tea consumer, the natural assumption is that China and Japan must feel the change of condition very severely. As a matter of fact, the merchants of these countries are the only material losers.

The greater part of China Tea sold was, and is produced by small planters who have never been able to secure an adequate price for their leaves, so when the demand for their tea fell off, many of them planted more beans and potatoes, and were just as well contented.

Japan has really fared better in the struggle, and has succeeded China as the principal source of the Green Tea consumed in this country, and supplied until recently almost half of the total quantity of all the Tea imported. Ceylon, India and Java Tea importations are now recognized as prime factors in the Tea business of America.

The titles most familiar to the public are, Black, in various qualities and prices; English Breakfast, generally a China Congou. (As a matter of fact, English Breakfast is a misnomer. Congous and some blends are called or named English Breakfast, which is simply an American trade term unknown in England).

Ceylon, Indias and Javas are black; mixed are blends of black and green leaves. Oolong: Green-Black leaf or Semi-Black or Semi-Green. Green Teas: "Gunpowder," "Young Hyson" and other sizes, and Japan in general usage applied to light Japan Green Tea.

The more "Fancy" varieties include the Pekoe, Orange Pekoe and scented types.

The titles popularly known, however, are entirely inadequate to describe or classify the many varieties of Tea on the market. They leave the importer, wholesaler or retailer a wide range from which to select varieties and blends to suit his trade and environment.

Even the list following China, Japan, Ceylon,

India, Java and other Teas is far from being exhaustive. It includes only the most important, and most generally accepted, trade titles and distinctions. Accuracy is rendered the more difficult by the lack of system in applying and retaining titles. Perhaps the widest range in titles is found in China Teas. They vary from very choice types, which are too expensive to make importation profitable, to large quantities of grades so poor and so badly manipulated that their importation into this country is not permitted.

Teas, as retailed, consist usually of several varieties or grades "blended" to produce the most pleasing results. A small quantity of an expensive, highly fragrant tea being added to a plainer, lower grade to improve its flavor; and over-strong high grade being toned down by a lighter variety, and so on indefinitely.

Note. See China and Japan Tea Articles.

CEYLON TEAS

The ordinary grades of Ceylon Tea are largely marketed in this country as "Ceylon Tea" of first quality, second quantity, etc.

A fuller division is into the following principal varieties, each subject to sub-division into several grades.

The best qualities are grown at high altitudes, the higher the better.

In Ceylon some of the most exquisitely flavored Tea comes from what is known as the Newera Eliya (pronounced Nuralia) district, the altitude of which averages about 6000 feet above sea level. These Teas are purchased entirely for their aristocratic flavor, as they carry but little strength.

Dimbula district with an altitude of about 4000 feet produces among the very best all-round Teas. They are not so flavory as the Newera Eliya Teas, but they possess a combination of flavor, strength and keeping qualities, which no other district in Ceylon equals.

"Broken Orange" Pekos or Flowery Pekoe," the very finest variety; the smallest and choicest young leaves from the top of the bush and a large proportion of golden tips, and produces a strong, powerful liquor.

This grade is not generally marketed here because the United States laws proh'bit the entry of any Tea containing more than a certain percentage of broken leaf that will pass through a certain designated sieve. As Broken Orange Pekoe is always small in leaf and contains a considerable proportion of still smaller tea, it must be very carefully screened if it is to pass the test, and the loss and difficulty thus involved, prevent all but the very largest importers from attempting it. The intent of the act when passed was to guard the public against inferior and unclean grades, but it has also resulted in keeping out some very choice types.

Orange Pekoe: Similar to Broken Orange Pekos, but the leaves are larger and there is a smaller percentage of tips of good appearance and quite free from small leaf or dust; the liquor is clean and fragrant and flavory, but not so powerful nor so aristocratic a type as the former.

Pekoe: The leaf is slender, whitish and satiny. The liquor is dark-reddish, but bright and fragrant.

The word Pekoe comes from the Chinese "Pak-Ho" meaning "Silver-Hair." In the old China variety of Tea, the bud-leaf and the end of the first leaf, produced when manufactured, a tip of silver color and of a hairy appearance, hence the Chinese called it "Pak-Ho."

This is the standard grade of Ceylon, also India and Java Tea used in America, and usually designates a good medium Tea supplying good leaf and liquor.

Broken Pekoe means just that, a Pekoe: leaf

108

slender, whitish, satiny; broken, hence **Broken Pekoe.** This cups very much like **Pekoe.**

Pekoe Souchong and **Souchong** constituting the bulk of the **Ceylon Teas** of general consumption, blended frequently with **Pekoe.** The leaf is larger and coarser than the preceding varieties, but give a rich and pleasant liquor.

It is the **black** varieties of **Ceylons** that have made for popularity. However, some **Green Ceylon** is also prepared under titles, corresponding to those of **China Green.**

Ceylon Teas are further divided by shippers into "low" and "high" grown, those from low ground and those from higher altitudes. The latter are much superior.

INDIA TEAS

The greater part of the India product is of the **Black Tea,** the best qualities generally coming from the **Darjeeling** and **Assam** districts. The leaf is ordinarily a gray-black, and is, in the best grades, **golden tipped.** The liquor is strong and pleasantly pungent.

Darjelling: The finest and most delicately flavored of the India Teas. It is grown chiefly in the **Himalaya Mountains, India,** at an elevation ranging from 2500 to 6500 feet. The leaf varies from the small, very tippy (Broken Orange Pekoe) to the coarse (Pekoe Souchong).

The first "flush" does not develop the special flavor of the Darjeeling. The second "flush", however, brings out this predominant characteristic, full, rich, flavor, and good keeping qualities.

Darjeeling "second flush" aid "Autumnal" growths are generally recognized as the finest the world produces, although equally as good Teas may be had in **Calcutta,** the supply is, however, rather limited.

There is no class of Tea in the world that brings

as high a price on an average, on the London market particularly.

Terai Teas: An India Tea but little known in America. It is very black in color, flat and irregular. Its decidedly fine cup quality makes it valuable for blending, it is of pronounced **Darjeeling** flavor. Terais are grown in Northern India, in the Terai district.

Assams: One of the high grade India Teas grown in the **Province** of Assam in **North-east British India.** It has a hard flinty, well made leaf of a dark greyish black color. In most cases carries plenty of Golden Tip and draws a full rich color liquor with a great deal of strength and pungency.

Assams in character are noted for their strength, fullnes and richness of liquor.

Dooars: A variety of Tea grown in the **Dooar** district, British India. This Tea has a soft mellow liquor, possesses strength, and a rich flavory cup quality. **Dooars** have not the style of the **Assams** in apearance, but are much sought after, and used largely in blending.

Travancores: Teas grown in the Province of **Travancore, Southern India.** This Tea very much resembles **Ceylon** Tea in appearance and character. It is a flavory Tea in the cup, with good strength, but is not very stylish in the leaf. As a rule, however, the better **Travancores** grown at an altitude of 5000 to 6000 feet naturally possess beautiful cup quality, and command good prices.

In many instances it is, indeed, difficult for even an expert judge of tea, to distinguish some of them from the high grown **Ceylon Teas.**

Owing to the geographical position, Teas from this **district** are marketed in **Colombo,** though the finer **Travancores** are shipped to **London,** and if not sold before reaching port, are sold at the **London auctions.**

Shylet Teas: A variety of Tea grown in the **Shylet district,** Assam, India. In style of leaf they very much resemble the **Assams** and **Dooars.** In the cup, however, they fall far short of either, for they lack strength, point and flavor, and usually produce a dull heavy liquor. Some of the Shylets, however, show a rich heavy liquor. These are frequently used in blends as a filler.

Cachar: The most common type, and is produced in the Cachar district of **Assam,** has rather an attractive leaf, but in the cup is flat, and lacks the distinctive flavor of the Assams or Dooars. However, **Cochars** are extensively marketed in America.

JAVA TEA

Teas grown in the Island of Java are handled very much the same as **India** and **Ceylon** Teas. They are manufactured by machine process, and are almost entirely of the black variety.

These are graded into Broken Orange Pekoe, Orange Pekoe, No. 1 and No. 2 Pekoe, Broken Pekoe, Pekoe Souchong and Souchong, Fannings and Dust. As in the case of **Ceylons,** they are known by the names of the gardens producing them.

Java Teas are further classified into **Assam Javas,** and **China Javas.** The former being raised from plants raised from **Assam** Tea seed, and the latter grown from plants raised from **China** Tea seed.

Assam Javas are in cup characteristic very much like the milder growths of Indias, while the **China Javas** show in the liquor the characteristics of the **China** Tea, both in developing the lighter color and in the flavor.

India Ceylon and **Java Teas** are graded and styled practically the same, as follows:

Flowery Orange Pekoe ..	Tippy, well made, wiry.
Flowery Broken Orange Pekoe	Tippy, even, clean, wiry.
Broken Orange Pekoe ...	Small, leafy, clean, broken (sometimes tippy).
Broken Pekoe	Small make, leafy, clean, even.
Orange Pekoe	Wiry, usually hard, clean, (tippy).
Pekoe	Boldish, black, well rolled, clean.
Flowery Pekoe	Few tips, boldish, black, clean.
Pekoe No. 2	Short, black, even, clean.
Souchong	Coarse, black, open (loose roll), clean.
Pekoe Souchong	Black, bold, clean.
Broken Pekoe Souchong or Broken Souchong	Short, black, broken.
Pekoe Fannings	Even, clean, small, flakey.
Fannings	Small, flakey.
Dust	Powdery.

Teas manufactured on all estates in these countries are graded in this manner. The grades do not indicate the cup quality of the Tea. The broken leaf makes a more syrupy or deeper liquoring cup of Tea than the wiry, hard-rolled, unbroken leaf, just as the ground Coffee makes a cup different to that made from the whole bean. The use of the broken leaf is more economical than the wiry leaf, because you can get the same strength of liquor with less leaf.

The English Tea drinking people know this, in consequence, use principally "broken" as has been stated.

CHINA TEAS

CHINA GREEN TEAS

The highest commercial types of "China Green Teas" are Moyunes and Teenkais. Others of importance are Hoochow, Fychow and Pingsuey.

Moyunes and Pingsueys were formerly principally distinguished by the color of the leaf. Pingsueys imported into the United States before the new law went into effect were a bright green, and Moyunes a dull gray. The Moyunes still retain their appearance, while the **Pingsueys** still have more the appearance of the **Moyunes**. **Pingsueys** still lend themselves to a better roll and cleaner apearance than the **Moyunes**, especially in the medium and lower grades.

Pingsueys, with the one exception of the very early teas, which are known as **Hoochows**, are one of the most important **China Green Teas**. However, they are made up largely for style, and to catch the eye, and are not as desirable in the cup as **Moyunes**.

The real distinction between **Moyunes** and **Pingsueys** is in the cup quality. The **Moyunes** have more cup character, body and flavor than the **Pingsueys**. However, **Hoochows**, (similar but a finer variety than first crop Pingsueys) and first crop **Pingsueys** are quite delicate in the cup, and far out-class the later **Pingsueys**, which become quite metallic in the drink.

All "China Green Teas" are graded as Fancy, Choice, Finest, Fine, Medium or Standard, as Nos. 1, 2, 3, 4 and 5. These are also sub-divided into: **Gunpowder**, consisting of the Youngest and Smallest leaves, roundish in appearance.

A rolled **China** made by sifting and hand rolling until they assume a shotty appearance, and where they are particularly fine, are frequently called **Pin-Head Gunpowder**. (Gunpowder style is also produced in the same manner of manipulation to a limited extent from India and **Ceylon** green Teas).

Imperial, like "Gunpowder" but larger. In three grades, first, second and third.

Young Hyson divided into five grades, Extra, First, Second, Third and "Cargo." The best grades have long well-twisted leaf, varying in size. **Hyson** larger than **Young Hyson** and more loosely twisted. In three grades, First, Second and Third.

Hyson is very similar to **Young Hyson**, only made from a rougher, bolder leaf.

The average consumer regards **Gunpowder, Hy-**

son, etc., as distinct qualities or varieties of Green Tea. Correctly speaking, they are the titles for particular sizes and shapes only. You may have Gunpowder size of the poorest or choicest.

Teenkais, Fychows and Wenchows are similar in leaf and cup, but inferior in quality to Moyunes.

Teenkais: A Tea district of China, producing rather attractive leafed Tea. The cup quality is not generally as desirable as that coming from the Moyune district.

Some Teenkais compare very favorably with Moyunes, but Fuchows and Wenchows are not as a whole as agreeable a drink as the Hoochows, and even first crop Pingsueys.

Moyunes, Teenkais, Wenchows, Pingsueys and Hoochows are graded: (1) common, (2) fair, (3) good, (4) fine, (5) finest, (6) choice, (7) choicest; according to leaf and quality

Country Greens: All China Greens other than Hoochows and Pinksuey.

Quite generally speaking, the principal China Green Teas as known to the trade are spoken of as Moyunes and Pingsueys. These are divided into Gunpowder, Imperial, Young Hyson and Hyson, or Hyson Skin. As before stated, the different names denote the style and make of the leaf.

Among other freaks in Tea is the Flowery Pekoe, the highest priced Tea produced in China, costing from 50c to $3.00 per pound, according to grade. It is a product of Foochow, and in appearance is a mass of Pekoe Tips, nearly white in color, and very light and fluffy. Only the terminal opening buds are plucked for this purpose. The cup quality is very light and characterless with almost no flavor, yet the Chinese who should be (and are perhaps) the best judges of Tea, use nearly all the better grades of the Flowery Pekoe produced.

114

These consist of **Oolongs** (?) **Congous** (so-called English Breakfast) and scented **Teas**.

Scented Orange Pekoe and Scented Caper: These may be considered under one head, as they are merely a separation by means of sifting out the different sized and shaped leaves. The straight or Young Hyson style leaf making the **Orange Pekoe,** and the round **Gunpowder** style gives us the **Caper.**

An ordinarily small leaf **Foochow** is used and fired by the usual semi-fermented method. At the end of the process, while the leaves are still hot, they are spread out and covered with a layer of Orange blossoms or Jessamine flowers, then another layer of Tea is spread over that, and the mass is allowed to stand until the flowers are wilted, when the flavor and aroma is absorbed by the Tea. The remains of the flowers are then sifted out and the Tea given another firing to remove the moisture absorbed from the flowers. It is then packed in 20-pound lead-lined Boxes or Chests, and is ready for shipment. The scent thus imparted to the Tea will be retained for years.

These Teas are used almost **exclusively** for **blending,** and are very useful for giving an attractive distinctive character to a blend difficult for a competitor to **match.** Only 10 to 15 per cent of Scented Tea is required to get a good result.

Oolongs are frequently classified as **Black Teas,** but they really constitute a separate type, for they are not as thoroughly fermented before firing as the general run of **Black Teas,** and therefore hold part of the flavor and a little of the color of **Green Teas.**

There are three recognized varieties, **Foochow, Formosa** and **Canton,** (a scented **China Orange Pekoe Tea**) but practically all of the supply imported is of the first two. **Formosa Oolong** in the choice grades, have evenly-curled leaf with a mixture of **Pekoe** tips; (2nd, 3rd and sometimes 4th leaf of the plant). It is very aromatic in flavor, which is delicate and is easily the most fragrant of Teas, the higher grades possessing a full, sweet bouquet, which is peculiarly characteristic of **Formosa Oolongs**.

Ning Yong: A China Tea district from which comes an Oolong Tea.

The various varieties of characters to be found in **Formosa** Teas are so great that it is quite as important to make a careful study of them as it is to be able to grade and select for value.

There is a vast difference between a **Formosa** made from a **Spring** Tea and made from a late **Summer** Tea, almost as much as the difference between a **Congou** and a **Ceylon**, or between a **Japan** and a **Young Hyson**, and there are various other reasons for vast difference, such as **climatic** conditions, systems used in **preparation, elevation, etc., etc.,** that often makes such a radical change in the cupping characteristics that, unless extreme care is used, the buyer is very apt to have some dissatisfied customers.

Early Spring or first-crop Spring Teas are very thin and light in the cup, but in some localities give excellent satisfaction as individual drinkers, and are used extensively with flavory **Ceylons** in blending.

Users of higher grades are particularly partial to the early Summer Teas, as they carry good body, handsome leaf and fine flavor. Teas picked later in the Summer (July) are showier and more tippy, and have a full, rich flavor.

You will find some of the medium grades in the late Summer picking that produce such a heavy liquor that a small proportion of **Ceylon** or **Congou** blended in will make a most excellent cup.

Usually the late Teas draw a heavy liquor, however, occasionally, strange as it may seem, you will pluck late Teas that have decidedly the characteristics of an early picking, both in appearance of leaf and quality in the cup.

The Black small leaf is usually selected in buying Choice Fancy Tea, as it in most cases stands for a better quality than the extra tippy leaf. What is sometimes termed the **Jessamine flavor** in these Teas quite likely originates from a slight reminder of the odor of **Jessamine Flowers,** frequently discernable in the cup, and it is a delicious cup too.

The **lower grades** are used principally for blending, and are good. Select your Teas for this purpose without dust or stems, and as little broken leaf as possible.

Formosa Teas are produced on the Island of Formosa, and are made up into Oolong. Formosa Tea being semi-fermented, has some of the characteristics of Black Tea, with certain of the cup qualities of the **Green Tea,** and therefore resembles a **blend** of the two. **Formosa Oolong** is delicate in flavor and fragrant.

Oolong is always a semi-fermented Tea that has been allowed to wither in the process of manufacture, and partially fermented. In this it differs from the **English Breakfast,** or **Congou** (Black) Teas, which are thoroughly fermented before being fired.

Foochow Oolong is especially black in leaf, and the liquor of the finer qualities is rich and mellow, but without as much body as **Formosa.** Ooolong, unlike any other variety of **China Tea,** is better in the **second crop,** or what is known as **Summer Tea.** The **Autumn Tea** has more merit than the average thirds of other Teas. Some of the first crops, however, are sweet in liquor and have a pleasant aroma. In all, there are four or five crops of Oolongs.

Oolongs are commercially graded as Fancy, Choicest, Choice, Finest, Fine, Superior, Good, Fair and Common. The bulk of **China Black Teas**

imported into the United States is known as Congou, (often called English Breakfast).

There are numerous grades, the highest of excellent cup quality, and their blending results in a great many varieties of all styles and values, among them numerous qualities of English Breakfast, Black Tea and Mixed Tea.

The principal commercial classifications are into Choice New-Crop, Choicest, Choice, Finest, Fine, Superior, Good, Fair and Common. By Nos. 1, 2, 3, 4, etc., and as Pekoe, Souchong, etc.

The leaf of the better qualities is greyish-black and well twisted, and the liquor is rich in color and pungently pleasant in flavor. Congous are usually classed as North and South China Teas, according to the districts from which they were shipped.

The North China Congous have, as a whole, more body than South Chinas. However, the better grades of South China Pan Yongs possess a good flavor and decided character.

Souchong: A corruption of the Chinese "Sianchung," meaning small plant. The old variety of Lapsang Souchong was produced from a small plant, and the growers invariably left this leaf to develop considerably before plucking. Consequently the Lapsang Souchong was always of a larger leaf than the other varieties of China Tea.

Indian planters appropriated this name for their largest leaf Teas; the first or smallest leaf was called Orange Pekoe, the second leaf was called Pekoe, the third was termed Pekoe Souchong, and the fourth or largest leaf was called Souchong. These terms are today applied to certain grades of India, Ceylon and Java Teas.

Souchongs: Term applied to certain large leaf Black Teas from South China. The liquor of these Teas is rich and syrupy. Some varieties have a smoky flavor, liked by many tea drinkers. They are seldom used in America, though very useful in fine China blends, giving them a distinctive character.

North China Congous are usually of a dull grey color, and of small curley leaf. The cheaper the grade the coarser the leaf as a rule.

Moning: A term which is applied to all North China Teas. There are many varieties, among them being Ningchow, Oonfa, Kintuck, Keemun, Ichang, etc.

Keemun: A fine grade North China black leaf Congou, of heavier body and not so stylish in appearance as the Ningchows.

The Ningchows and Keemun are the leading North China Blacks.

Kintuck: A variety of North China black leaf Congou. A flavory, full bodied, fine cupping Tea, very similar to Keemun.

Kalsow: A variety of South China Congou Tea generally low, medium grade and low priced.

South China Congous consist principally of Pan Yongs, Paklins and Packlums. The most desirable of these are the Pan Yongs. The dry leaf is black and coarser than the average Ningchow, but the leaf is generally good black, and the liquor delicate and flavory, of good body and character.

The Packlums are the most stylish in appearance of all China Black Teas, the leaf being small, evenly made and black. The better grades show considerable white tips; they are handsome, but lack body and character.

Packlin: A variety of South China black leaf Congou Tea. It has a well made, small black leaf. The liquor is dark red, but lacks character and flavor.

Prominent among the fancy Teas are: Flowery Pekoe: small, evenly folded, olive colored, generally scented, and carry a profusion of white velvety tps. Orange Pekoe: small, black leaf, with yellowish ends, generally scented. (Resemble Packlums in appearance). Pekoe: small, with whitish tips, generally scented. **Powchong:** (also used as a general term for all China paper package Tea) rather rough, dull black leaf; a variety of Teas, highly scented with the **Jessamine** flower, manufactured mainly for consumption in **China** and the **Philippines.**

Capers and **Koolaws** are also included in the scented Teas. **Capers** are shaped like **Gunpowder** or **Japan Nibs**, highly scented (Black) with a flavor similar to the **Scented Orange Pekoe.**

Scented Orange Pekoe: This is a variety of **China Souchong,** and is a highly scented Tea. Scented Teas are sometimes produced by sprays of Orange or other blossoms by being placed over the trays during the withering process.

The fragrance of **scented** Teas is not natural, but is imparted from flowers, seeds or roots, such as **Jessamine, Gardina, etc.** In some districts the scenting material is added during the firing process, and afterwards separated by sifting. The method used generally is this: The scenting material is pread over the top of the Tea after the Tea is prepared and ready for packing, (one pound of the leaves or blossoms being the usual proportion to each 100 pounds of Tea) and allowed to remain on the chest at least a day, until the Tea becomes thoroughly impregnated.

Scented Teas, as a whole, possess very little merit in the cup, being very light, without body or character. They are used principally for blending **Black Teas.** It is far better **not to use them at all,** as the natural flavor of Teas is best for the consumer. If used, they should be used sparingly, say one pound to twenty pounds.

Padraes: A South China **Red Leaf Congou,** known by its small red leaf.

Saryunes: A large red leaf **Tea** grown in the **Saryune** district of **China.** It produces a thick, heavy liquor, and is not unpleasant in the cup.

Tea is grown all over Japan. The system of cultivation and method of preparation is very similar to that of the Chinese.

The **first crop Teas** are best. The later the crop, the less merit to the cup; however, some of the later Teas have good characters. **First** picking begins about the end of **April** or the beginning of **May;** the second crop a month later, and the **third** crop in **July-August.** The better grades, notably those from the **Yenshy** district, possess a delicate rich flavor, peculiar to themselves; the lower grades are metallic.

Japan Teas are made up to preserve their natural quality, without fermentation or withering, and are therefore "**Green Teas.**" They are, however, known as **sun-dried, pan-fired, basket-fired** or **porcelain-fired.**

The best varieties of **Japan Teas** show a medium-sized or small leaf, and a bright, clear, fragrant liquor, the latter in the **Green Teas** generally of a lighter color than the **China Green.**

Formerly **Japan Teas** were divided into **Pan-fired, Sun-dried** and **Basket-fired.** Now they are simply divided into **Pan-fired** and **Basket-fired.** (Uncolored.)

Basket-fired: This is a term applied to **Japan** Tea, which has been cured in Baskets, by the firing process. The process consists of putting from seven to ten pounds of Tea into an hour-glass, shaped basket, having a sieve in the middle, by means of which the Tea is held in the upper part of the basket.

The basket is placed over a charcoal fire, and during the course of firing, which lasts about an hour, the basket is removed two or three times and the Tea turned over, thus insuring even fir'ng.

Pan-fired: The term applies to **Japan** Tea. As soon after the leaf is plucked it is steamed and certain juices extracted, after which it is rolled on a paper on a sheet-iron pan, over a charcoal fire to make it curl and to extract sufficient moisture to keep it until it can be shipped to the factory.

This process takes from forty minutes to one hour, the work being done near the plantation. Upon arrival at the factory the Tea is again placed in iron pans over charcoal fires and stirred with iron arms operated by machinery until properly cured. This re-firing takes from a half to one hour, according to the "toast" required.

(Porcelain-fired: Japan Tea, which has been fired in a similar manner to "Pan-fired,'" except that it is not rolled and manipulated to such an extent. It is consequently rougher in appearance than "Pan-fired," but there is less in weight by breakage, and it is consequently cheaper.

The name has no particular significance. It was aparently arbitrarily selected to make a distinction between this process and that of "Pan-firing."

Pan-fireds and Basket-fireds are produced from the same leaf, the only difference being in the method of handling and firing. However, some Teas are better adapted for Basket-fired than for Pan-fired Teas. The leaf is fired in pans over charcoal furnaces and prepared for export by machinery. The color of Pan-fired Tea is an olive-green. (Formerly light-green).

Basket-fired, as the name would indicate, is a Tea fired in baskets. Japan Tea in the raw state looks like Basket-fired, but the Spiderleg varieties are rolled and styled up to please the eye.

Spider Japan or Spiderleg: A long, thin, handsome, straight leaf, tightly and stylishly twisted Basket-fired Japan Tea.

Natural Leaf Teas: These Teas are all from the Kawani, Hachioji and Momikiri districts, and in appearance of leaf are between the Basket-fired and Pan-fired. They are fired on paper trays in interior, and sometimes re-fired in pans or baskets.

Spring Teas: Term applied to Japan and Formosa Teas, plucked in the April and May season.

Summer Teas: Japan and Formosa Teas gathered in the season from June to September.

Autumn Teas: Japan and Formosa Teas plucked in October or later.

Classification: Japan Teas are classed as Yokohama Teas and Kobe Teas, according to the districts from which they come.

Kobe Teas: The Teas which are shipped from the districts which constitute Kobe Teas are, as a whole, inferior to the Yokohama Teas, but some of the higher grades are very sweet in the cup.

Yokohama Teas: Teas shipped from Yokohama are grown chiefly in two great districts, Suruga and Yenshu. These two districts might again be divided into several smaller ones, the Teas from which vary slightly in general character.

Yenshu: In this district are produced the best drinking Teas of Japan, notably in the Kawani Hachioji and Momikiri sections. As a rule, the Yenshus have not the style of the Suruga Teas. The characteristics of this Tea is a straight, long, flat leaf, the liquor being light in color, but rich in flavor.

Suruga Teas: These are the stylish Teas of Japan. From this district comes the greater proportion of what are known as Spiderleg Teas. They are also made up into Pan-fired.

Kawani: A small Tea district in Japan producing a fine quality small leaf Tea. The liquor is rich and rather light in color.

Momikiri: A comparatively new make of Japan Tea, generally made of the high grades of Tea from the Yenshu and Kawani districts. It has rather a small clean leaf, and cups well.

Surugas are noted for the handsome and stylish appearance of the prepared leaf. They lack the fine cupping quality of the **Yenshu,** the liquor being very often grassy in flavor.

After the firing process, the Tea is sifted and graded to match the various standards to fill import orders; on importation they are graded as: **Pan-fired:** medium size, 'generally green, evenly curled. **Basket-fired:** long, dark, well twisted.

Dust or **Fannings.**

"Nibs" is irregularly twisted, larger leaf, sifted from the higher grades.

For commercial purposes, **Japan Teas** are graded as **Extra-Choice, Choicest, Choice, Fine, Good, Medium** and **Common.**

They are marketed both as **Japan Teas** No. 1, No. 2, No. 3, etc., and by conventional titles for size and style.

BRICK TEA

This consists of Tea leaves and Tea leaf dust. The term applies particularly to **China Tea, Japan Tea,** however, is also made up into bricks. Brick Tea is manufactured by using usually three grades of Tea for each brick. The Tea dust is moistened, usually by steam after having been placed in a mold. Each mold has a layer of the fine or medium Tea at the top and bottom, with a coarser grade in between. It is subjected to a pressure applied by a power of from 15 to 25 tons per square inch.

This pressure is applied to the whole brick, it is only applied for a very short time when the mould is locked with wedges and kept so for two or three hours.

The bricks usually weigh about 2½ pounds each and measure about 1 x 6 x 7 inihes in size. Three or four weeks are usually required for the bricks to dry.

These are manufactured extensively for local consumption in various sections, and for export to **Tibet, Siberia** and elsewhere.

The **Tea Caddy** is a small chest, box or canister or a chest containing several canisters, for packing or holding Tea. **Caddy** was adapted from the **Chinese catty,** a small measure of Tea, as a characteristic title for Oriental Tea packages themselves.

Catty was derived from the **Malay kati,** a fraction more than a pound.

Large quantities of imitation Oriental Caddies are now made in this country, and used by Grocers to re-pack Tea. They are shipped in "nests," the smaller sizes fitting into the larger, thus giving a wide variety of sizes and occupying very little space.

When used as a measure, the word "caddy" now generally signifies any package containing less than a half chest. A **Chinese** chest is equivalent to about 82 pounds or three-fifths of a Pecul (about 139 pounds).

The **India** and **Ceylon** chests contain 90 to 140 pounds.

Chests: The original Tea package, usually made of wood and lined with lead. Generally speaking, while **India** and **Ceylon Teas** are packed in "chests" and sometimes in "half chests," other Teas come mostly in "half chests."

"**Chests**" of **India** Tea weigh from 110 to 140 pounds; "**Chests**" of **Ceylon** Teas weigh from 90 to 110 pounds.

Tea Tablets: Consist of Tea Dust or finely ground Tea pressed into cubes or squares for use in the open by hunters, campers, etc.

Tile Tea: Is a kind of flat **Brick Tea** made in **China,** exported via **Keachti** and distributed throughout **Siberia** and **Tartars.** It is cooked with milk, butter, salt and herbs, and eaten as a vegetable.

Thick Teas: Indias, Ceylon, Javas, Congous possessed of a full, strong, heavy liquoring "draw." Hence the application "Thick Tea."

The Tea industry in the United States has never reached noticeable proportions or received much comment, although for perhaps a hundred years various atempts have been made to establish tea-growing gardens in this country, these have been successful in a very limited way.

Pinehurst, (Gardens) Summerville, South Caro lina, has produced some Teas of excellent quality, however, they have not met with any degree of commercial success. The United States Department of Agriculture has made extensive experiments with India, Ceylon and China Tea seed, and have the satisfaction of realizing a small but growing output of Black and Green Teas each year, but they have not yet entered into competition with the Asiatic crop.

Pinehurst Teas: Grown on a garden by that name at Somerville, South Carolina.

TEA BLENDING

You have undoubtedly used the term "blend" very frequently in referring to Tea. In fact, it may very well be that you have "blended" Teas among your own brands. This use of a blend is very common, and two or more kinds of Tea blended in a skillful manner result satisfactorily to the consumer and profitably to the dealer. The object is not, as the public may sometimes imagine, to lower the quality, or reduce the cost to the dealer, but simply to produce a better Tea, and to obtain a finer and more desirable flavor than that yielded by any single variety. Thus a Tea may be suitable in flavor, but lacking in body, or light in liquor. By adding to it one or two other Teas possessing these qualities, the defect is remedied and a full-flavored, heavy-bodied Tea is produced, to the greater satisfaction of the consumer.

The art of "blending" Tea has been highly developed in England, but the average Tea man in the United States has only a superficial knowledge of Tea blending. This is a most interesting and important department of the Tea business, which may well be studied and developed.

Unquestionably the highest branch of the Tea business is in the blending of Teas. The mixing of different types, styles and strength to produce or acquire special results.

The successful blending of Teas can only be accomplished through patience and close practical application, and is usually brought about by the use of proper proportions of light and heavy, aromatic and flat, and stylish and low grade Teas, black for blacks and green for greens as a rule. However, blends are sometimes built from a combination of blacks and greens, All blends should, first: Be constructed to produce a desirable cup; second: Price is a prime factor. A good example for instance is: A high type Darjeeling, a full bodied Assam, and a good grade Dooar and a Newera Eliya Ceylon proportioned possibly as follows: 20% Darjeeling, 30% Assam 20% Dooar, 30% Ceylon would construct a very desirable blend.

To produce a better cup (which would, of course, cost more money), increase the amount of Darjeeling and Ceylon, reducing the amount of Assams correspondingly.

By proper manipulation, you should be enabled to build a good blend with a wide range of price, and still maintain excellent cup quality. Very much the same result can be obtained by the use of a good Ceylon type of Java Tea, leaving out the Ceylon. This would, ordinarily, reduce the cost considerably without reducing the cup quality to any noticeable extent.

All types of Teas, fermented, unfermented, and even semi-fermented, have to be handled in this manner in blending to obtain the result sought.

To produce a particularly pleasing **blend** is not an easy matter, and to repeat it is still more difficult. In other words, a reproduction of a blend and maintaining same year after year from the crops of different seasons, requires experience, extreme patience and honesty of purpose, concentration, hard work, and last, but not least, a **good nose** and a sensitive, delicate sense of **taste.** It is most undesirable to establish a demand for a particular flavor in your blend if you are not capable of keeping it up.

The Tea business is really an art, and is very fascinating, and profitable if successfully conducted.

Tea, whether in package or bulk, should **never** be kept in the **sunlight,** nor near any article or articles of **distinctive odors,** and its place of storage should always be perfectly **dry** and moderately **cool.**

Tea naturally keeps fresh best in tight-fitting canisters, and in sealed tin or lead packages, but it deteriorates with age, no matter how it is packed.

HELPFUL HINTS ON TASTING, TESTING, BLENDING AND SELLING

An ideal location to be selected for a testing room for either **Teas** or **Coffees** is one with an unobstructed northern light. This affords the best opportunity for close scrutiny—a light that shows you the best and the worst.

In all **Black** and **Semi-Black** (semi-fermented) Teas there is to be found a percentage of flaky leaf, more or less yellow, which is very noticeable in a strong light, and might be readily overlooked under less favorable conditions. This is an inferior leaf, and not only affects the style, but is good evidence (except in **Japan Teas**) that an inferior quality has been added. This would have a tendency, of course, to lessen the value of the Tea. In consequence, the utmost care should be used to ascertain to just what extent these leaves have been introduced. :

In testing **blends** or 'blended Teas, it is always well ito' taste from several drawings; in order to determine the thoroughness of the mixing. Should there be a pronounced difference in the cup of the different "draws" you will readily understand that, while your **blend** may be all right, your various types are not properly, or evenly, mixed.

A small, hard, well-rolled, uniform leaf is usually accepted for style, but without a good light, one is quite apt to misjudge the size, and texture, particularly if the Tea is highly colored, in which case color and polish might prove deceptive and cause the important qualities, such as make, hardness and uniformity to be overlooked.

Frequently the best "drawings" from **Black Teas** are from those that show no tips whatever, although many buyers are prone to take them into serious consideration. There is no question but what a small, black, hard, well-twisted, uniform-leafed **Formosa** is superior to a coarse, uneven leaf with any amount of tips. The same may be said of the choicest **Darjeeling,** for those sold at the fanciest prices are of the classy black leaf.

In testing for **cup quality,** a counter or table, or even a bench of convenient height may be used. The dry tea leaves are weighed out and placed in cups or small china pots, each holding one cup of Tea. Fresh **boiling water** is then poured on. Some then cover the **cups** with a saucer or the pots with a lid, and let stand for five minutes; others do not cover but begin at once to use the nose, and as soon as the liquor is "up"; tasting begins.

The infused leaf is usually removed, however. The inspection and comparison of the infused and dry leaves may be conducted very intelligently by lifting the infused leaf in the spoon.

An expert can, of course, get more information from a minute examination of the infused leaf than the beginner. E. G., he can take a **Congou** (said to be one of the most difficult Teas to grade correctly) and not only get a good idea of the grade, but can tell positively whether it is new or old-crop Tea, and even if it is first or second-crop, and frequently assure himself just what district the Tea is from. The choice and preference in **Congous** is usually given the Teas of bright, copper-colored, infused leaf over the dull and darker shades. The same is true in all **black** or **semi-fermented** Teas, and to some extent all kinds of Teas.

In testing Tea (or Coffee) your sight is used largely to keep you from wasting time; your sense of **taste** and **smell** are of the utmost importance.

Your **sight** will show you the difference in appearance of liquor, say between the **China** and **Indian** Tea, or **China** and **Java** Teas.

Your **sight** will also show you the difference between the infused and the dry leaf, and will teach you what to look for in testing. The infused leaf of a good Tea should be a rich yellow or "old gold", while the poorer Tea leaf infused is usually dark and dull.

Your **taste** will show you the decided difference between, say, the flavor of an **India** Tea and that of a **China** Tea. Taste the Tea (hot) by sipping from a dessert spoon, letting it rest on the tongue for an instant, then spitting it out. (Do not swallow Tea or Coffee in your regular testing work.)

Your **taste** (with some practice) will teach you the difference in liquors from **Indian**, **Ceylon**, **Javas**, etc.

Always cleanse the mouth well before tasting. Rinse with water and soda, or take a bite or two of apple, or a slice of lemon.

Your sense of **smell** used in conjunction with your sense of **taste** helps you to distinguish the Aroma, and more fully appreciate the flavor, and combined add much to the important factors of memory and recognition.

You can not know Teas (nor Coffees) without studying, testing them along the lines of **tasting**, but by constant **sight, taste,** and **smell** you can become an expert.

TEA ANALYSIS, AND ITS USE AS A BEVERAGE

The most important components of the Tea-leaf are **theine** (the chief stimulating principle), $2\frac{1}{2}\%$ to $3\frac{1}{2}\%$; **second,** the oil and resinous ingredients, which furnish the flavor and aroma of the liquid; **third,** the gummy substances and the tannin, which give it "body" and strength. There is in addition a small quantity of essential oil, which slightly increases its stimulating properties.

Tea also carries, according to chemical analysis, 40% to 60% protein, cellulose, fibre, etc., but nearly all of this is found in the Tea leaves left after pouring off the liquid. The greater part of the tannin (from 12% to 18%) also becomes a part of the residue, assuming, of course, that the Tea is made fresh, as it should be.

To obtain the best results, **fresh boiling** water must be used,; the pot must be kept hot (but not **boiling),** for from three to five minutes after pouring the water on the leaves; the Tea should not stand longer than five minutes before drinking.

If the water used is not fresh, that is, if it has been standing long, or has ben previously boiled, the Tea will be insiped and flat in flavor.

If the water is **not boiling** when poured on the leaves, it will produce a rough, raw-tasting liquor. An earthenware pot is better than a metal one. Putting the dry Tea leaves into a pot well warmed produces a better result than putting them in a cold pot.

The fresh-brewed liquor, after four or five minutes' infusion, contains almost the total amount of Theine (identical with Caffeine in Coffee), and only enough tannin and associating components to give it palatable strength.

If the liquid is allowed to stand on the leaves longer than five minutes, the flavor will be injured by the extra tannin produced; seven or eight minutes, and the tannin not only detracts from the flavor, but the liquor becomes pungent, acts as an astringent, and in consequence becomes very detrimental to digestion. The liquid can be saved, however, if poured off the leaves into a fresh china or earthenware vessel.

India, Ceylon and Java Teas are, as a rule, considerably stronger than China and Japan. Individual tastes differ also, hence the quantity of leaves to be used must be judged entirely by the requirements.

The water in some localities will make much better Tea (also Coffee) than water in other places. It is claimed by some authorities that soft water should be used when brewing the more delicate types, and that where the water contains lime or other mineral matter to excess, stronger, coarser and heavier Tea leaves should be used.

Again some experts assert that the "best Tea" is the best everywhere. However, the experience of the writer rather tends to varify the former statement.

In making iced Tea, use at least one-fourth more leaves than for Tea to be served hot; use the same care, and do not allow the liquor on the leaves more than six or seven minutes; then pour off into another vessel and allow to cool very slowly. It should be made three hours before it is to be served. This gives ample time to cool gradually. Tea suddenly chilled, either by ice or refrigeration, spoils the flavor beyond a doubt.

When ready to serve, add ice, sugar, lemon, etc., according to taste.

U. S. SHOULD DOUBLE ITS TEA CONSUMPTION

Every man who depends upon the Tea business for his livelihood must feel dissatisfied with himself whenever he considers the deplorable fact that we, in this prosperous country, consume only one pound of Tea per capita yearly. With Australia using 9 pounds per capita, Great Britain 6 pounds, and Canada, just across the border, consuming over 4 pounds, all people with similar habits and ideals and speaking the same language, we certainly should be able to double our present consumption. If we could do that the business would be much more worth while for all engaged in it.

TABLE OF THE PRINCIPAL KINDS OF TEAS AND THE REPRESENTATIVE TEA-GROWING DISTRICTS OF THE WORLD.

CHINA

China Greens (Shanghai)

Country Greens

Cup Qualities	Grading for All Country Greens
Moyunes (Nankin, Pakheong, and Hyson Liquored).	Moyunes: Fancy, Choice, Finest, Fine, Medium, Standard.
Teen Kais.	Teen Kais: Fancy, Choice, Finest, Fine, Medium, Standard.
Fychows.	Fychows: (Smoky Teas not admitted to the United States).
Soeyoens.	
Wenchows.	Soeyoens.
Local Packs.	Wenchows, and Local Packs.

Hoochows Ping Sueys.
  Style or Make:
Pin Heads.
Extra Gunpowder.
First Gunpowder.
Second Gunpowder.
Third Gunpowder.
First Pea Leaf.
Second Pea Leaf.
First Young Leaf.
First Young Hyson.
Second Young Hyson.

CHINA CONGOUS (Black)

(So-Called English Breakfast)

South China

(Red Leaf Congou)

Kaisow.
Cheong-lok.
Chick-Sowkai.
Ching-wo.
Saryune.
Soumoo.
Sin-Chune.
Suey-Kut.
Yung-How.
Yung-Tong. (Choice to choicest, fine to finest, good to superior, fair.)
Paklin.
Paklum.
Panyong.

North China

(Black Leaf Congous)

Moning.
Ning-chow.
Ke-mun.
Ichang.
Kin-tuk.
Confa.
Oonam.
Chun Sowkai.
Yung Low Tung.
Oopak.
Liling.
Kutoan.
Ho-How.
Sunntan.

Other Congous

Campoi.
Canton.
Hoyune.
Padrae.
Pekoe.
Pouchong.
Qui-fa.
Tayshan.

Souchongs

(Seldom used in America)
Canton. (New Make or Macaos.)
Lapsing. (Foochow-Louchong.)
Oolong-Souchong.
Padrae.
Pekoe.
Tenmow-quefn. (Choicest, extra fine to finest, superior to fine, common to fair.)
Panyong.

Scented Teas

Capers.
Pekoes.
Powchongs (Foochows, Cantons, Macaos).
Pekoes: Pekoe, Orange Pekoe, Flowery Pekoe, Hung-muey.
Pouchongs: Pouchong, Pouchong-Pekoe,

Padra-Pouchong.
Canton Scented.
("Congee.")
Macao.
China Oolong (Black)
Amoy: Kokews, Mohea,
Ningyong, Ankois, Bo-
hea.
Foochow: Saryune, String
Teas. (Choicest to
Choice, Finest, Fine,
Superior, Good, Fair.)
Brands "Chops": Tong-
mow, Tong-lee, Tong-
shing, Chun-fa, Shun-

fat, Sun-kee, Cheng-ke,
Cum-wo and Cum-wo-
kut.
Suey Kut.
Ching Wo.
Tycon.
Panyong.
Padrae.
Pekoe-Oolong.

Various

Mandarin.
Compressed.
Fannings.
Dust.

INDASIA

(India, Ceylon, Java)

Northern India
Districts

Assam.
Darjeeling.
Dooars.
Punjab.
Dehra-Dun.
Kangra.
Kumaon.
Sylhet.
Cachar.
Madras.
Nilgirns.
Terai.
Chittagong.
Travancore. (Southern
India.)

India Greens
Uncolored

Young Hyson.
  (1st and 2nd.)
Hyson. (1st and 2nd.)
Fannings.
Dust.
Gradings: India (Black)
Broken Orange-Pekoe.
Orange-Pekoe.
Flowery Orange-Pekoe.
Pekoe.
Pekoe-Souchong.
Souchong.
Fannings.
Dust.

India Greens
Colored

Gunpowder. (1st and 2nd.)
Imperial. (1st and 2nd.)
Young Hyson.
  (1st and 2nd.)
Sow Mee.
Hyson. (1st and 2nd.)

CEYLON

Black	Green
Broken Orange Pekoe.	Gunpowder. (1st and 2nd.)
Orange Pekoe.	Imperial. (1st and 2nd.)
Flowery Orange Pekoe.	Young Hyson.
Pekoe (1st and 2nd.)	(1st and 2nd.)
Broken Pekoe.	Hyson. (1st and 2nd.)
Pekoe Souchong.	Dust and Siftings. (Choice
Broken Pekoe Souchong.	to Fancy, Fair to Good.)
Fannings.	
Dust.	

JAVA

Black	Green
Pekoe.	Imperial.
Pekoe-Souchong.	Hyson.
Congou.	Young Hyson.
Oolong.	

JAPAN AND FORMOSA

Japan	Formosa Oolong
Pan-fired.	(Tamsui)
Sun-dried.	Fancy, Choicest.
Basket-fired.	Choice, Finest.
Porcelain-fired.	Fine, Fully Superior.
	Superior, Fully Good.
Gradings	Good Cargo, Fair.
Extra-choicest.	Cargo, Common.
Choicest.	
Choice.	**Leading Districts**
Finest.	Chap Ko Hoon.
Fine.	Pai 'chie.
Good Medium.	Sinteam.
Good Common.	Chuitngka.
Common.	

OTHER COUNTRIES

UNITED STATES	Natal Africa
South Carolina	Golden Pekoe.
(Pinehurst Tea Estate)	Pekoe Souchong.
Souchong.	Flowery Pekoe.
Oolong.	Souchong, and other
Sun-cured.	Chinese-named Blacks.
Shelter.	
Green.	
Compressed Tablets.	

Note.—Divers China Teas included in this list are either too low-grade to be allowed entry to the United States, or too expensive for export, consequently unknown to the general trade. There are also some couple of hundred or so plants here and there about the Globe which are, or have been, used locally for making "tea-like" infusions, as the "Camomile Tea" of Germany, the "Cowslip Tea" of the British, the "Teamsters' Tea" of Arizona, the "Revolution Tea" of New Jersey, the "Coffee-leaf Tea" of Indasia, etc. There are estimated to be some three thousand tea brands, blends, trade-names, trade-marks, package-names, etc., in the world.

WORTH REMEMBERING

It is well to **bear in mind that all Tea** is produced from the **same shrub (or tree)**, conditions being responsible for the various types: altitude, country, soil, season, preparation, etc.

Theine: Is an alkaloidal substance found in the Tea leaf, chemically identical with Caffeine (of Coffee). The Theine content of Tea averages 2%.

Tea Taster: An expert judge of the cup quality of the leaf; one who judges Tea by testing in the cup and in the hand.

Cha Si (Chinese): An American or English Tea tester—the most important man in the "hong" factory, field or garden.

Chop: A "Chop o' Tea" is a collection of a number of lines of Tea under one brand name, and may consist of one or many more of various grades.

Line: A line of Tea consists of one grade in a "Chop," usually about eighty "half chests," but may be more or less.

String Teas: South China Tea made into Oolong.

137

This Tea is always very carefully and heavily fired, and has a heavy burnt flavor.

Broker: A Tea broker is one who negotiates the sale of Tea from one dealer to another, for the consideration of a brokerage from the seller. The brokerage is usually 2% on general business, and 1% on invoices.

As said before, the better grades of Dooars and Assams are rich, heavy liquoring Teas, but do not approach the Darjeeling in flavor and aroma.

Teas are principally grown in the following countries: India, Ceylon, Java, Sumatra, China, Japan and Formosa. (It is also grown in small quantities in South Africa, and in a very limited way in South Carolina, U. S. A.)

Each of the principal Tea-growing countries produce several different grades of the two varieties marketed, namely fermented or Black, and unfermented or Green.

Tea-Consuming Countries, and the amount consumed per capita annually: Australia uses 8½ to 9 pounds per capita, England uses 6½ to 7 pounds per capita, Canada uses 5 pounds per capital, Russia uses 2½ pounds per capita, United States uses not quite 1 pound per capita.

In Great Britain, "Brokens" are used almost exclusively.

The origin of some Tea names: "Gunpowder" Tea is claimed Anglo-Saxon. The name was originally suggested by its small, round, shot-like form. The Chinese call it "Pearl Tea" or "Choo-Cha."

It would seem that nearly all Tea titles now in use were originally of Chinese origin. However, most of them are corruptions. E. G. "Congou" from "Kung-Fu" (Labor). "Souchong" from "Siau-Chung" (small sprouts). "Pekoe" from "Pak-Ho" (white hair), referring to the down on the young leaves.

"Young Hyson" from "Yu-Tsien" (before the rains) or (young spring-time).

"Hyson" from "Hetsien" (spring-time), the season of the first and second picking.

"Oolong" from "Ou-Loung (black dragon), no doubt referring to the black leaves mixed with the yellowish green.

Imperial: Derives its name from its resemblance to Tea used in the Imperial household, and is sometimes called "Big Gunpowder."

Denatured Tea: Tea which the English customs deem unfit, for consumption. This is mixed with lime and asafetida and marked "denatured." In this way the Theine or Caffeine content is extracted and used in medicines.

Dust: The powdery and smallest siftings from the sieving process, being leaf practically reduced to powder. Importation of this class of Tea is practically forbidden into the United States.

India Teas are called the "Bergundy of Teas." They differ somewhat from Ceylon, being deep black, and the latter a dark brown.

They are stronger than Ceylon, due, it is said, to soil fertilization and to the fact that the juice that is expressed from them in the fermentation process is put back. (?)

TEA IMPORTS, PRICE AND CONSUMPTION

Five Year Averages—1851-1914

| Period. | Net Imports | | Import Price Per Lb. Cents. | Per Capita Consumption. Pounds. |
	Quantity. Pounds.	Value. Dollars.		
1851-55....	19,476,000	5,254,000	27.16	760
1856-60....	22,578,000	5,461,000	24.64	758
1861-65....	24,814,000	6,265,000	24.56	.740
1866-70....	39,973,000	11,670,000	29.22	1.080
1871-75....	57,090,000	20,643,000	36.08	1.368
1876-80....	61,981,000	16,454,000	26.60	1.302
1881-85....	70,471,000	16,185,000	22.70	1.316
1886-90....	82,597,000	13,956,000	17.02	1.376
1891-95....	89,675,000	13,676,000	15.52	1.340
1896-00....	86,217,000	11,356,000	13.20	1.186
1901-05....	95,814,000	13,848,000	14.20	1.162
1906-10....	93,594,000	15,210,000	16.24	1.036
1911-14....	95,954,000	17,200,000	18.00	980

The Maté tree grows from ten to fifteen feet in height, and produces leaves resembling those of a pear tree; is considered a species of Holly. It is used universally in Brazil, also in other parts of South America, as a beverage, which corresponds to the "Tea" of other countries.

The leaves are ground to a coarse powder, sometimes, but more frequently of late years the leaves and small young shoots or twigs are simply broken, ranging from coarse to fine, with as small a percentage of powder as possible.

Maté is prepared very much in the same manner as our "Tea," and may be taken with sugar and cream, although it seems to be more popular clear, as it is preferred extremely hot.

Where the powdered form is used (and this is still the popular form in many districts), the beverage is taken through a small tube called a "Bombilla." Drinking tubes with strainer at lower end, shaped very much like a deep teaspoon (possibly not quite so large), with the flat side or top covered and perforated with very fine holes. The tube is possibly as large as an ordinary lead pencil, and as long or longer. The upper end is slightly flat. Bombillas are made from silver and other metals, and, as stated, are used in universal Maté (native willow Tea) drinking principally in South American countries.

One end of this tube is in the form of a bulb pierced with very fine holes. This acts as a strainer and prevents the powder and other particles from being sucked up into the mouth. The Germans, however, in preparing the beverage bring it to a good boil and then dash cold water into it, in sufficient quantities to stop the boiling. The leaves or powder settle and the Maté may then be taken as pure and in the ordinary way.

The effect of Maté as a beverage is restorative and stimulating. The component parts are very similar to Tea and Coffee, including an important percentage of their stimulating principles. (Theine and Caffeine.)

Maté or Yerba Maté (ilex paragueyensis). The consumption is enormous throughout the Latin Republics—averaging about 14 pounds per capita, or nearly double the per capita tea-consumption of Australasia. All attempts to introduce Maté among northern races have proved commercial failures.

Spices: Are described as aromatic vegetable substances used chiefly to season food; different portions of their respective plants are used. **Ginger** comes from the root of the plant, **Cinnamon** the bark, **Cloves, Nutmeg,** etc., represent the fruit, and **Sage, Thyme** and other herbs the entire upper part of the plant.

Their essential oils are chiefly responsible for their aroma and characteristic qualities.

Tropical **Spices,** such as **Pepper, Ginger, Nutmeg, Cloves,** and **Cinnamon** were, because of their great scarcity, even more highly regarded in olden times than they are now. They are quite frequently referred to in the Old Testament, and are there generally classed with other items of considerable value, in fact, they were considered valuable and fit presents for the royal families.

It is a matter of record that these spices were a part of the tribute which other monarchs paid to Solomon. The wealthy Romans were especially lavish in their use, in the preparation of food. Also at the altars and at funerals burned with Incense.

Arabia was popularly credited with being the home of all spice luxuries in ancient times and through the middle ages, but this was largely due to the fact that it served as a market for spicers or spice merchants from the East India Islands, particularly Ceylon. As time advances, we find that the trade occupies an important position in the history of our present civilization. For a long period of years pepper was one of the principal items of commerce between India and Europe. Venice and Genoa, and other cities, became wealthy largely through its traffic. Frequently rents were paid in pepper, and occasionally a tax was levied.

Cloves, Cinnamon and Nutmeg are responsible for a much darker chapter, cloaking many deeds of blood-satin and atrocity.

The **Portuguese** and the **Dutch** for generations maintained their control of the supply by executing any but government employees attempting to engage in its export, by destroying plantations and accumulated stores and on several occasions by massacring entire native populations to prevent them selling to other nations.

On the beginning of a more progressive enlightenment, the destruction of monopoly control and the scientific cultivation of various spice plants, have brought an abundance of all varieties at prices which transform former luxuries into an every-day possibility for even the poorest classes.

Extensive substituting and adulterations were practiced in modern commercialism, for, until quite recently, a large proportion of "Spices" sold were mixed with other materials that greatly reduced their strength, impaired their natural flavor and greatly injured the legitimacy of the **Spice** business; but conditions have greatly improved in recent years and both retailers and consumers can now, by exercising a little judgment, secure pure high-grade **Spices** of every kind.

This improvement has had a decided tendency to restore a confidence in the public, and in consequence the demand has been greatly stimulated. This will prove very profitable to the merchant who takes advantage of the changed situation by using special care in purchasing good stocks and devoting more time and space to displaying and explaining them where necessary. There is a nicer profit in handling **Spice** than in most grocery items. There is a wide field for their use; in consequence, there is enormous quantities used.

All **Spices,** particularly **ground** Spices, should be protected from exposure of any nature by keeping in tightly-closed receptacles.

The principal **Spices** of general modern consumption are **Pepper, Ginger, Cinnamon, Cloves, Allspice,** or **Pimiento, Cayenne Pepper, Mustard,**

Cassia, Bay. Leaves, Anise, Capers, Celery Seed, Cardamon, Caraway, Dill, Fennel Caraway, Coriander ·Horseradish, Sage, Paprika, Nutmeg, Mace, Marjoram, Turmeric, Thyme and Savory. Several of these are known as sweet herbs. However, they are all Spices and so classified and recognized in government and analytical circles.

Nutmeg: The Nutmeg is the kernel of the fruit of a tropical tree, native to Asia, Africa and South America.

The pink or red flesh covering it is the almost equally popular Spice known as Mace.

The whole fruit is about as large as a peach, and of a yellowish-green color. It is, in the East Indies, often preserved entire as a sweetmeat.

The tree begins bearing at the age of eight years, and continues to yield for about seventy-five years. It carries ripe fruit at all seasons, but there are three principal harvest periods: July, when the fruit is most abundant though yielding thin Mace, November, when the fruit is thickest but the Nutmegs are small, and March, when both Nutmeg and Mace attain their finest condition, but the total product is less in quantity, on account of the dryness of the season.

After the Nutmegs have been gathered and stripped of their outer covering they are placed upon gratings over slow fires and dried at a slow heat, not over 140° F., until the kernel rattles freely in the shell.

The shells are next cracked and removed, and the kernels sprinkled with lime, to protect them from the attacks of insects, and to destroy their power of germination, and then packed for export in tight casks, previously soaked and coated on the inside with lime wash. In this condition they will keep for an indefinite length of time.

In purchasing Nutmegs, choose those which are round and compact in shape, of oily appearance and heavy.

They are graded and quoted by the number to the pound, varying from 80 to 140. The largest are the more showy, but those of moderate size, other points being equal, are just as good (even better for grinding).

Light, dried, dull kinds, or those of long, oval shape, should be avoided.

The bulk of the United States' supply, which is more than the total consumption of all other countries combined, comes from **Penang** and **Celebes,** of the **East Indies.** There is also a small, steady importation from the **British West Indies.**

Mace: In the inner covering which envelopes the **Nutmeg.** It closely resembles a lacerated membrane, being blood-red and somewhat fleshy when fresh. It is prepared for market by being fully flattened out and dried for several days in the sun, much of it becomes red-yellowish during process. It is used both in "blade" and ground form to spice soups, sauces, pudding, etc., its flavor closely resembling **Nutmeg,** but being, to many tastes, even more pleasing. It also furnishes a strong, yellow, volatile oil, and a red, buttery, fixed oil, which, mixed with other substances, is known as **Nutmeg Balsam.**

The bulk of the supply comes from **Bandi** (the best), **Penang, Singapore, Celebes,** and, though only to a comparatively small extent, the **West Indies.**

Care should be taken to choose that with a deep **orange color** and clear, transparent, wax-like appearance. Dull-looking parcels are not desirable.

"Macassar," "Papua" and **"Bombay" Mace** are fiictitious titles sometimes given to a wild product, the mixing of which with cultivated **Mace** is rated adulteration.

Mace should always be kept in airtight, glass bottles or tin boxes.

Penang Spices: A term occasionally applied to a mixture of various spices, employed in cooking, preserving, etc.

Cloves, widely used for flavoring desserts and confectionery, and medicinally, are the dried flower buds of the Clove tree. As packed, they are reddish in color, but this changes to the familiar dark-brown in the process of drying, performed either by the smoke of wood fires or by exposure to the sun.

The Clove tree, an evergreen, grows to a height of forty feet, bears its developed Clove buds in its seventh year, and gives two crops annually, increasing its productiveness up to an age of nearly a hundred years.

The average yield per tree is about five pounds of Clove buds. In the initial drying there is usually 50% loss in weight and another 8% to 10% is lost in shipment to Europe or America.

Fully two-thirds of the Clove crop is produced at Zanzibar, and its neighboring Island of Pemba, but the quality is much inferior to the Penang and Amboyna prouct. The most desirable Clove is the full-sized brown, plump bud, and the Penang is considered the finest on the market. Amboynas are also high grade and very desirable. The Zanzibars, owing probably to the inferior methods of drying and collecting, are often shriveled and black.

The Clove industry was for many centuries conturies confined to very narrow limits. A few Islands of the Molucco group furnished the world's supply up to the beginning of the seventeenth century; then the Dutch, having driven the Portuguese out of the "Spice Islands," tried to destroy all the Clove trees except those on the Island of Amboyna, to perfect their monopoly.

Later the Island of Zanzibar became an important producer, but for a number of years following 1872 it was again unproductive, as the result of a cyclone, which uprooted nearly all of the mature fruit-bearing trees.

An interesting result of the cyclone was the release from the **Dutch Government** warehouse at **Amboyna** of surplus **Cloves** that had been accumulating there for generations, no sales having been permitted except when the bids reached the prices set by the Government. The markings on some of the barrels received at that time in **New York** showed that they belonged to the surplus of crops reaching back nearly a hundred years. Some of the barrels were ready to fall to pieces, but the **Cloves** were in **excellent condition.**

The principal sources of supply today are the Islands of **Zanzibar** and **Pemba** (**British, East Africa**), and the **East** Indies (both **Dutch** and **British**).

The best grade of **British** is that known as **Penang;** that of **Dutch** is **Amboyna.** Dark, well-formed **Cloves** are the best.

Mother Cloves is the dry, ripe fruit. It somewhat resembles the olive in appearance. Its flavor is similar, too, but much weaker than that of the ordinary **Clove.** They contain little oil and are not suitable as a spice. Planters further hold that the growth of the **Mother Clove** exhausts the tree, so, therefore, as few as possible are left when the picking season is over.

Allspice, also called **Pimiento** and **Jamaica pepper,** is the dried fruit of a small **West Indian** tree called the **Pimiento.**

It is about the size of a pepper, or small pea, and is gathered when fully grown, but not ripened, and dried in the sun. It is called **Allspice** from its supposed resemblance in flavor to a mixture of Cinnamon, Nutmeg and Cloves. It is often used in place of Cinnamon.

Cinnamon is the spicy bark of young branches of the **Cinnamon tree,** cut off in strips and dried in the sun, curling during the process into the quills with which the consumer is familiar.

Ceylon Cinnamon is obtained from **Cinnamomum Zeylanicum**, native to **Ceylon** but also cultivated to some extent in the **East Indies.** **Cassia Cinnamon** is from **Cannamomum Cassia**, the chief **East Indian** and **Chinese** type.

Both kinds are sold both in quills and ground, their fragrant, aromatic flavor making them a popular adjunct in cookery, confectionery, etc.

Ceylon Cinnamon is the variety referred to in the general article on **Spices**, as, in earlier days, a commodity of great value and the cause of many wars and much bloodshed. It was first carried to the world's markets by **Arabs**, who kept its source a great secret for a number of centuries, and contrived to discourage possible investigation by stories of fabulous monsters inhabiting the country from which they were supposed to obtain it. That the tree grew wild in Ceylon was not generally known until the fourteenth century, in spite of the fact that the spice had been continuously in use since the early days of **Israel**, **Greece** and **Rome**.

Ceylon Cinnamon is of a pale yellowish-brown color and generally of lighter, cleaner and smoother appearance than **Cassia**.

The quills (the smaller enclosed in the larger) are also usually thinner and more tightly rolled, but these distinctions are not absolute, as there are many grades of **Cassia**.

Cassia Cinnamon was until recent years decried as an inferior imitation, principally because the greater part of the supply consisted of the inferior and poorly prepared **China** product. It has, however, just as good botanical title to the general name of "Cinnamon" as the **Ceylon** type, as the result of the fine quality now exported from **French Cochin-China** and the **Dutch East Indies.** It is today given the preference in the **United States** and in several **European** countries, because its flavor is more pronounced and more lasting. The **Ceylon** is milder and so much more volatile that it loses readily on exposure to the air.

The demand for **Ceylon Cinnamon** has indeed so lessened that commercial interests are urging the cultivation of **Cassia** in **Ceylon** in order to maintain the Island's position in the trade.

In analytical circles, the **Ceylon** variety is still conservatively described as "**True Cinnamon**" instead of the commercial term "**Ceylon Cinnamon.**"

The lower grades of **Cassia** are cheaper than any of the **Ceylon** generally marketed, but the best qualities are more expensive.

The four **main grades** are those known as **Saigon,** or **Saigan,** from **French Cochin-China** (the choicest); **Corinche** and **Batavia** of the **Dutch East Indies** and **China** (the cheapest). **Saigon Cassia** is generally used for blending with lower grades.

PEPPER

The **Black** or **White** powdered **Pepper** used as a condiment is the ground fruit of the **Piper Nïgrum,** (**L**) a perennial climbing shrub, native to the forests of **Western** and **Southern India,** but for centuries cultivated also on the **Maylon Peninsula** and in **Sumatra, Java Ceylon** and **Siam,** and to a limited extent in **Borneo** and various other **Tropical** countries.

The fruit is a small, round berry, the **Pepper** in loosely-packed clusters of from twenty to thirty, closely attached to a common fruit stalk, a good vine producing an annual average of from one to two pounds.

Pieces of the stalk may often be found in whole **black Pepper** and examination will show the depressions formed where the berries were attached.

The shrub or vine grows to a height of eight to twelve feet, and is supported either by poles or trees. The "Peppercorns" are exported in bags of 64 to 128 pounds.

Black Pepper consists of the dried, immature berries of the shrub, gathered as soon as one or two on the clusters commence to turn red.

After removal from the stem they are dried in the sun or near a mild fire, the outer fleshy portion of the berry, shriveling in the process, turning brown or black and becoming hard, brittle and adherent to the stony, inner portion, thus forming a hardened, wrinkled cortex.

Among the principal commercial varieties listed in a recent Government report are: **Malabar** (Mangalore, **Tellicherry,** Alleppy, etc.), **Singapore,** Penang and Trang, **Acheen** (or **Sumatra** or **West Coast**), and **Lampong** (or **East Coast**), named either from the place of cultivation or that of shipment.

Malabar Peppers are those from the **Malabar Coast of India.** "Mangalore" peppercorns are very large, twice the size of ordinary pepper, of a deep black, very clean and uniform, giving, when ground, a powder of greenish-black appearance.

Tellicherry Pepper is that grown on the **Malay** Peninsula, principally in the Southern extremity known as the **State of Jahore.** It constitutes a considerable portion of all the pepper raised, and, because of its dark color and fairly uniform quality, is a product of good appearance. It is not, however, so highly regarded for grinding purposes, because of its smoky odor. The pepper and gambier plantations of **Jahore** are usually under one management, and the pepper is dried by placing it on mats suspended over the kettles in which the gambier is boiled down to make the vegetable extract. The smoke from the furnace underneath dries the pepper, but at the same time imparts to it a decidedly smoky smell, which is retained to a considerable degree, even after the pepper is ground. It is, indeed, one of the tests by which the pepper merchant determines whether a given sample is **Singapore** or not.

Trang and **Penang Pepper,** shipped from **Penang,** is grown in either **Java** or **Sumatra.** It is of especially rich color.

Acheen, Sumatra or **West Coast** are names applied to the pepper obtained from Acheen, the western extremity of the **Island** of **Sumatra.**

Lampong Pepper or **East Coast** is grown on the east end of the **Island** of **Sumatra,** near the **Straits** of **Sunda.**

As a rule, the heavier the **Peppercorns** for size, the better the grade. They should be firm and round, clean and uniform in appearance and not too much furrowed.

Acheen Pepper has been standardized by general agreement, and the four chief grades are now determined by their specific gravity. Classed: A. B. C. D. B weighs a little less than A, C less than B, and D less than C. Dust not to exceed 3% in any class.

The many advantages of this method will probably result in its extension to all Black Peppers in the near future.

The other varieties described in this work are generally superior to Acheen, and give much higher results on the weight test. For example, A grade **Acheen** weighs 4 lbs. and 13 ozs. to the **Imperial Gallon,** while A grade **Alleppey** sometimes weighs as much as 6 lbs. and 12 ozs. and contains practically no dust.

Tellicherry ranges from 6 lbs. to 6 lbs. 12 ozs., and is equally clean.. **Lampong** averages about 6 lbs. with a dust percentage of 1½% to 3%, and **Singapore** from 5 lbs. 5s ozs. to 5 lbs. 8 ozs., the dust ranging up to 4%.

White **Pepper** is practically the same product as **Black Pepper**, except that the outer shell or pericarp of the berry is removed to a greater or less extent by friction, following soaking in water. It is sometimes made at the plantations, but just as frequently by manufacturers who buy the **Peppercorns** in the open market.

Some manufacturers prefer, for White **Pepper**, berries that have been allowed to ripen before picking, as they are more easily decorticated, but this is not a universal rule.

Decorticated White Pepper is the term applied to the product which, in addition to losing the outer dark shell, has also had the seed-coats partly or entirely removed.

There are numerous qualities to the length to which the process has been carried. The most expensive is that from which all three seed-coats have been removed, producing smooth, hard, pearly kernels. Other grades retain one or two seed-coats.

There are several grades of **White Pepper** on the market, corresponding in a general way with **Black Pepper**, such as **Singapore, Penang, Tellicherry, Siam, etc.**

Coriander White Pepper is a product of especially attractive appearance, screened to uniform size and then bleached.

Shotted Pepper: Polished in a cylinder and sometimes slightly oiled to present a polished, glazed appearance.

Mignonette Pepper: A term sometimes applied to coarsely-ground Peppercorns.

Pepper shells is the by-product of external shell or cuticle obtained in the manufacture of White **Pepper.**

Ground Pepper, whether **Black** or **White**, should consist only of whole or hulled peppercorns reduced to proper fineness by grinding and sieving.

152

Long Pepper is chiefly derived from wild plants of the genus Chavico Miq. The fruit spikes. gathered when green, are cylindrical in form and cov-, ered with closely packed, small, round berries. The product is crudely prepared, the berries hardened together with and adhering to the woody stem, and generally including a large quantity of dirt and other extraneous matter. It does not possess the fine flavor or strength of true pepper, and its addition is rated as adulteration. Its principal use is for pickles.

CAPSICUMS

Red Pepper, Chilies, Cayenne Pepper (sometimes called Guinea Pepper), Paprika.

These are the most widely cultivated Spices in the world. We are told that originally the plants were natives of South and Central America, and the various names used in the different sections of the Globe seem to prove this assertion.

The seeds are easily transported, 'and have therefore been brought to almost every country for cultivation.

The growth is most favorable in the warmer climates, and the crop is always in large demand by the natives in the fresh state as a vegetable.

Red Pepper is the powdered ripe pod, both flesh and seeds, of any variety of Capsicum, the plant which gives us the edible fresh "pepper," but which bears no relation to the true pepper-plant.

The most noted varieties are cultivated extensively in the East and West Indies, Mexico and the Southern States.

Cayenne Pepper is distinguished from Red Pepper in general by its dull red or brick red color, as compared to the brighter red of Red Pepper.

Napaul and many other Cayenne Peppers are extremely light-colored, as they should naturally be if properly made from the ground seeds alone, unmixed with the redder husks of the fruit capsules. Hence, the lighter color and milder flavor' of genuine Cayenne Pepper.

Capsicum Seeds after the removal of the pericarp and thoroughly washed and dried are entirely devoid of acridity and pungency.

The best-known commercial varieties are Zanzibar, Mombassa, Sierra Lecone and Japan, the last named being less pungent than the others. Named after Cayenne, a city of French Guiana.

Napaul Pepper is from a capsicum grown in Nepaul, India. It is a choice variety of Cayenne Pepper, yellowish-red and very pungent, but of especially agreeable flavor.

Cayenne is a powerful stimulant, producing a sense of heat in the stomach and a general glow throughout the body without narcotic effect. In small amounts it is an aid to digestion, particularly of vegetables, which partly accounts for its general use in warm weather.

Paprika, also called Hungarian Pepper and Sweet Cayenne Pepper, is the powdered flesh (only) of a long, fruited variety of common Capsicum, grown principally in Hungary and Spain, but also to an increasing extent here. It is red and mildly pungent.

The several grades are determined by the selection of the peppers and their treatment, both before and after grinding. Pods of especially reddish color and mild flavor are considered the choicest. Sharpness of taste denotes inferiority.

Paprika is a very valuable Spice for flavoring dishes, and is almost universally liked even on the first use. It should always be kept dry.

Chili, or Chiles: The Mexican, and quite generally the popular name for the pods of several species of small-fruited, specially pungent Capsicums, put up as a separate pickle or added to

154

"mixed pickles," etc. They are largely consumed in hot countries.

, The two **Mexican** dishes containing them which are best known here are **Chili-Con-Carne** and the **Chicken Tamale.** The word is also used as a group name for many articles highly seasoned either with whole Capsicums or Cayenne Pepper, etc.

The **Japan Chili** is a bright-red fruit, about three-quarters of an inch long. There is a **Japan Chili** imported which averages about one and one-quarter inches long, but the smaller size is usually preferred. This article is the favorite in the pickling trade, and is also used in the grind to lend a bright color to **Cayenne Pepper.** It does not passess as much strength as some other grades of Chilies, and is not usually ground alone.

The usual original trade package is a pocket of 50 or 100 pounds.

The **Mombassa** Chili is a fruit about one-half inch in length, of a browninsh-red color, and is considered the strongest grinding chili on the market today.

The original package is also either a 50 or 100-pound pocket.

The **Bombay Capsicum** is a pod about two or three inches long with a thick skin and a heavy stem. It is usually the cheapest grade available for grinding, and if a lot of bright, red, clean pods are secured, will produce a good colored powder of considerable strength.

The **Bombay Capsicum** is mixed with **Mombassa** or other strong **Chilies** by many grinders to produce a strong, ground **red Pepper** at a moderate price

To the native of India Spices and condiments are indispensable. Dr. Watts says: "He will eat contentedly by the stream-side a meal of uncooked flour and water, provided it is flavored with a few green Chilies."

155

Most shipments of the article arrive in bales of about 240 pounds each.

Japan Capsicums are similar to the **Bombay** in size, but have a less heavy skin and usually a lesser proportion of stem. They do not make a strong grind, and are used chiefly in mixture with stronger grades to produce a ground **red Pepper**.

The **Bombay Cherry (Pepper)** is a blunt cylindrical fruit, about three-quarters of an inch in length, bright red color and free from stem. It possesses fair strength and makes a good-colored, desirable grind.

The usual package is a bale of about 240 pounds.

The loss in weight from the grind of **red Pepper** is considerable and owing to the moisture in some grades, many millers have trouble in preparing their product.

There is a diversity of opinion as to what constitutes a **Cayenne** and what a **red Pepper,** the common idea being that the product of a grind of any **Capsicum** produces either.

In the writer's opinion the same standard should govern either or both, as the laymen knows no such fine difference, but desires the one article, whether he refers to it as **Cayenne** or **red Pepper.**

Chili Tepine: A small round red to yellowish-red pepper, pleasantly pungent, about the size of an ordinary pea. Grown in **Mexico, South** and **Central America.** Perhaps more extensively, however, in Mexico than elsewhere. Used principally for flavoring **meats, fish, soups,** etc.

Tabasco: A long-podded red pepper (also short and also green), cultivated chiefly in Southern Louisiana.

It is best known to commerce as **Tabasco Pepper Cause,** a rich, red, concentrated extract; generally put up in small bottles with corks shaped for dropping. It is also sold powdered, but to less extent.

Tabasco Sauce is excellent for flavoring soups, salads, etc, and some people like it on oysters, fish and meats. Only small quantities should be used, as it is very strong. In making sauces, etc., if a sharp, quick effect is desired, mix with vinegar. If otherwise, mix first with olive oil and salt, and then with vinegar, the result will be soft and delicate, but still strongly marked by the characteristic Tabasco flavor.

TABASCO PEPPER CULTURE

How the Tabasco Variety Is Grown and Prepared for the Market

This description of the methods pursued in the cultivation and preparation of peppers for the market refers to a particular type of Tabasco Pepper grown in the parishes bordering the bank of the River Teche, in Louisiana. The details are furnished by the Creole Pepper Company of New Orleans.

"The soil along the banks of the Teche," says this grower and packer, "seems to possess what is necessary to mature the 'green' flavor which tabasco peppers alone possess."

"Attempts have been made to increase the acreage by raising the peppers from the same seed, in other parishes, but while the peppers were 'attractive' to the eye, and 'hot' to the palate, they lacked the peculiar flavor of the genuine Tabasco, grown in the Teche country."

"Three varieties are cured, known as the 'Green,' large and small, 'Red' Tabasco Peppers. The 'green' are firm and will keep indefinitely when properly cured and constantly covered with brine. Perhaps they possess more of the bona fide tabasco flavor than do the 'red,' and they are not quite so pungently hot. This 'green' tabasco is quite a favorite with the Creole epicures, who use them on the same plate with their dinners."

"The crop is a costly one, and the plants are delicate shrubs. Severe winds, which come every now and then; excessive rains, or early cold weather, all have an important bearing on the annual crop, the gathering of which begins in August and continues until November."

"The peppers are gathered mainly by women and children. They are preferably picked in the early morning, and they must be, at the curing plant and in the brine within six hours from the time they have been taken from the bushes, and the peppers remain in this brine solution, consisting of nothing but salt and water, until they have been sufficiently cured. This process takes from four days to a week, according to the weather conditions prevailing at the time."

Capsicum. There are many species of Capsicum, all natives to the warm parts of **America, Africa** and **Asia,** and now cultivated in every part of the world. The small-fruited types, generally the most pungent, are best known popularly as **"Chilies,"** and the larger as **"Peppers."**

Chilies are used whole in vinegars, pickles, etc., for making popular hot dishes, and to grind into **Cayenne Pepper,** and **"Peppers"** are eaten as a vegetable, and ground into **Red Pepper** and **Paprika.**

MUSTARD

The **Mustard** in general use as a condiment consists of the crushed seeds of the **Mustard** plant, native to **England,** but capable of almost universal cultivation.

The mature plant ranges from three to six feet in height, and has bright-yellow flowers. There are two chief varieties, the **white,** producing pale-yellow seeds, and the **black,** with seeds smaller, more irregular and dark brown on the outside, though also **yellow** inside.

In trade circles, the products are distinguished as "Yellow and "Brown," but there is little difference in composition, and the retail product is generally a mixture of the two.

Mustard was used medicinally by the most celebrated physicians of antiquity.

As a condiment it dates from the latter part' of the sixteenth century, but it was little known until the year 1729, when an old woman of the name of **Clements,** residing in **Durham, England,** began to grind the seed in a mill and to pass the flour through the several processes necessary to free it from the husks. She kept her secret for many years, selling large quantities throughout the country, especially in **London.** The product obtained the name of **Durham Mustard,** from her residence in that city.

The manufacture of **Mustard** at first consisted essentially of grinding the seed into a very fine flour, a bushel of seed weighing sixty pounds yielding only twenty-eight to thirty pounds of **flour Mustard.**

Manufacturers soon discovered that they could please the public palate better by modifying the pungency of the flavor, and the result is that today it is made in a great variety of styles, each establishment following its own formula for mellowing, blending, mixing, etc. Genuine **Mustard** is easily obtainable, but it does not please the general taste as well as the prepared, modified article.

In moistening or "mixing" dry mustard, or mustard flour, two main objects must be kept in view. First, to obtain the desired consistency. Second, to make it perfectly smooth. To produce these effects, add the liquid in small quantities and rub and pound the mustard well with a spoon. The simplest form of preparation consists of mustard flour, moistened with sufficient water to produce the consistency of thick batter, with half a teaspoonful of salt added for each two ounces of

mustard flour. Some people like the fine, powdered sugar included in the same proportion as
salt. Vinegar and Olive Oil can be used according
to taste, but some cold water is necessary for the
first mixing in order to develop the pungency.

If, for immediate use, milk, or milk and cream,
may be employed in place of either vinegar or oil.

The greatest part of the prepared mustard now
enjoying popular use and favor consists of 50%
to 75% vinegar, flour thickening and various condiments.

U. S. prepared mustard is a paste composed of
a mixture of ground Mustard Seed or Mustard
Flour, Salt, Spices and Vinegar

GINGER

Ginger (Hanbury says it was well known in
England prior to the Norman Conquest), in its
commercial form is the root-stock of the **Ginger**
plant, a perennial reed-like plant with annual leafy
stems, three or four feet high, which grows freely
in moist places in all tropical climates.

The root is gathered when the stalk withers and
is immediately scalded, or washed and scraped;
in order to kill it and prevent sprouting.

The former method, applied generally to the
older and poorer roots, produces black **Ginger**.
The latter gives white **Ginger**.

The natural color of the "white" scraped **Ginger**
is a pale-buff. It is often whitened by bleaching
or liming, but generally at the expense of some of
its real value.

White **Ginger** of the first grade should be large,
light-buff throughout, soft and even in cutting and
of strong characteristic flavor. The present supply comes chiefly from **Jamaica**, the **Malabar Coast**
of India and the **East Indies**. "Cochin" and "Cali-
cut" are titles borrowed from the two Indian cities
of those names.

African Ginger is dark, but has an excellent, strong flavor. Borneo Ginger is merely a former trade term for some white Ginger. None is exported from Borneo.

Japan Ginger, usually bleached or limed before shipment, is of fine appearance, large and smooth, but is much inferior in strength to the other varieties mentioned.

Preserved or conserved or Canton Ginger consists of young, green roots boiled and cured in syrup and put in pots and jars. The principal consumption is of the imported Chinese product, but there is an increasing sale of West Indian.

Crystalized Ginger is also made from the younger roots. The best grades from roots selected for uniform size and appearance are called "Stem Ginger."

Medicinally, Ginger, as Jamaica Ginger, etc., is a grateful stimulant and carminative, being much used for dyspepsia, colic, etc. It is also frequently employed to disguise the taste of nauseous medicines. Ginger Tea is an old-fashioned remedy for colds.

"Switchell' is a summer drink, once very popular in the haying fields, made from Ginger, molasses and water, with a little vinegar added to give it acidity.

Condiments: Substances taken with food to season or improve the flavor, or to render it more wholesome or digestable. They include such articles of general consumption as Salt, Vinegar, Spices, etc. A majority of them in moderation, stimulate both appetite and digestion, but their excessive use tends to vitiate the gastric juice and injure the stomach.

Poultry Seasoning: A preparation of spices and herbs ready mixed for use in stuffing fouls. It sells easily during the Fall and Winter Hollidays.

SEEDS

Corinader Seed: The fruit of a small plant
growing chiefly in the South of Europe. It is
used as a culinary flavor, especially for curries, in
confectionery, and to aromatise spirituous liquors.

Dill:. An herb of the parsley family, grown
chiefly for its aromatic, pungent seeds, which are
employed in the manufacture of sauces, pickles,
etc.

Cardamon: The dark, wrinkled, triangular seeds
of a spice plant native to India. They possess an
aromatic and agreeably pungent flavor and are
used in cooking, especially in curries and soups,
by confectioners, etc.

Anise Seed: The minute seeds of an annual
plant, cultivated chiefly in Spain, Egypt, Syria and
other Mediterranean countries, but also to a large
extent in Germany, principally in the vicinity of
Erfurt. It is used as a condiment, in the manufacture of liquors, candy, etc.

Star or Chinese Anise, imported mainly from
China, is in flavor similar to common Anise, but
is very different in appearance, being star-shaped
and frequently of a total diameter of about an
inch.

Caraway Seed: The highly aromatic seeds of
a plant which grows wild in the meadows of Holland, and Northern Germany, and is cultivated in
many other countries, including the United States,
especially California.

They are employed in a variety of ways, as a
culinary flavor, in confectionery, baking, etc., and
in the perfumery and soap-making industries.

The roots of the Caraway plant were at one
time eaten as a vegetable, and the young and
tender leaves still occasionally serve for flavoring
soups, etc.

Hemp Seed: Commercially is best known as a
food for canaries and other cage birds. The plant
is an annual, of the nettle family, and attains an

average height of from four to eight feet, is grown chiefly in India, **Russia, Argentina**, and the **United States.**

Rape Seed: Also known as **Cole Seeds.** These are used for bird food, both straight and mixed with other seeds; is a member of the turnip family.

Poppy or **"Maw-Seed"** of both the **Black, Blue** and White **Poppy**, is retailed to some extent for use on or in bread, generally of the Vienna shape and rolls, such as the **German "Salt-Stangen."** Analysis show about 50% oil, and 25% protein and pectins.

It is also sold as bird food, then frequently styled **Maw-Seed**, and is considered an especially desirable diet when birds are moulting.

Rape Seed comes from the **Rape** plant, a member of the **Turnip** family, cultivated in both **Europe** and **Asia.**

Rape Oil is obtained from the **Rape Seed**, and is used chiefly in the manufacture of soap.

Millet: Is the smallest of grains, but is very abundant in product, each plant having a number of stalks and a single head, sometimes giving two ounces of seed.

Common Millet, the variety chiefly cultivated in this country, is broadly divided into **brown** and **yellow** grain. The former, used in the same manner as **rice**, makes good puddings, but the greater part of the domestic crop of all types is used as green fodder, although there is large quantities cured, stacked or stored and fed to stock as hay.

The ripe **seeds** are also valuable as bird and poultry food.

Imported Millet, in Germany and Italy, consumed in large quantities in soups and other forms, is of smaller grain types than **Common Millet.**

The yellow **Italian** is used here to some extent for puddings, but the bulk of the supply is retailed as food for cage birds.

Another variety, known as **Guinea Maize**, is

common in **Peru,** furnishing there white flour of very pleasing flavor.

Canary Seed: The seed of the **Canary Grass,** **native** to the **Canary Islands,** but long ago naturalized in many temperate climates. Its principal use in this country is as bird food. It is generally mixed with **Rape** and other seed to cheapen it, but the straight **Canary** seed is decidedly preferable.

It should be kept in a dry place and away from vermin.

Industrially, a flour made from **Canary seed** is employed in the manufacture of fine cotton goods and silk stuffs, and in the **Canary Islands,** Italy and **North Africa** is used as food.

SPICES, HERB AND SEED (ology)

In this case Cummin, Cumin, Cuminas, or Cominos is the "cause of it all" (particularly at this time).

The writer has seen this **herb, seed** or **spice** listed by jobbers, brokers and druggists, and spelled variously, as above.

This is an "herb" that produces a "seed" that is classed as a "spice." It is of the **Caraway** type. The seeds have an aromatic odor and taste which makes it popular as a flavoring for soups, pastry and so forth. It is, and always has been, particularly popular in Europe and the **Far East.**

It is used quite extensively in the United States, its greatest use perhaps being in **Curry Powders.**

Curry Powder, or Curry Paste: Is a condiment so highly seasoned that it is only within recent years that it has obtained a substantial foothold in temperate climates, though it has been used extensively in India and other **Eastern** countries for many generations.

In India it generally consists of **Black Pepper, Cayenne Pepper** and a variety of Spices—**Cinnamon, Nutmeg, Cloves,** etc.—made into a **paste** or **powder** with Turmeric.

Its composition varies with different makers.

That sold here usually contains chiefly Turmeric, Coriander Seed, Cayenne, Black Pepper, Fenngreek Seed, Ginger and Lime juice. It is handled in jars, bottles, packages, etc.

The word "curry" is of (Asiatic) Indian origin, and originally signified there a "stew"—generally of chicken, veal or lamb.

The "finishing" or seasoning of the dish used to be quite frequently performed at the table by the host or some other member of the party; later, the word came to be applied more particularly to a mixture of Spices.

In India and Ceylon, curry sauces are added to a variety of dishes, generally a few minutes before serving or before the completion of the cooking. Vegetables of all kinds, in addition to meats, poultry and fish, are so treated. Curry is best kept in a bottle or jar tightly corked.

Fenngreek: Is an herb which resembles clover. Its seeds (as just mentioned) are used as an ingredient of Curry Powder; separately, they are strong, bitter and of unpleasant flavor.

Turmeric: Is the yellow root-stock of a plant of the Ginger family, marketed both in root form and as a powder. It is the principal ingredient in Curry Powders, and is also used for mixing with Mustard and other spices. Its yellow color, after the extraction known as Curcuma Oil and Curcummin, is employed as a dye-stuff in chemistry, etc.

HERBS

Basil: A highly aromatic herb, with a flavor resembling cloves. The common variety is seldom made use of, but there is a large type whose leaves are employed very generally in flavoring sauces and soups, especially green and mock turtle soup.

Basil Vinegar is made by steeping the leaves in vinegar.

Bay Leaves: The leaves of a shrub of the Laurel variety, growing wild in **Greece**, Italy and other **Mediterranean** countries and in some **Southern** sections of the United States.

Among the ancient **Greeks,** the **Bay Leaf** was in large part dedicated to heroism and poetry, but modern usage consecrates it to the more material pleasures of the table. The principal consumption is of the dried leaf, used as flavoring for soups, etc.

Myrtle: A small evergreen tree, whose sweet, pulpy and aromatic black berries are dried for use as a condiment, in addition to their consumption fresh. Both leaves and wood also yield an oil used in the manufacture of perfumes.

Bergamont (an herb), a title frequently applied to a family of several different plants used for their stimulating and aromatic properties, as "wild Bergamont," "American Horse Mint," etc.

Marjoram: A garden herb of the **Aster** family. There are numerous varieties, the most desirable being the **Sweet or "Knotted,"** Winter **Sweet** and **Pot.** Both the tops and leaves, green and dried, are used to flavor soups, dressing, etc.

For drying, the branches are cut before the flowers open, marketed in leaf and powdered form.

Common or Wild Marjoram grows wild in many parts of the country in the open fields. It resembles the cultivated types, but is coarser in flavor.

Oregano or Mexican Marjoram: Grows wild in **Mexico** and **Central America,** is sometimes cultivated in a small way in the former country. The whole or powdered leaves of this plant are pleasantly pungent, slightly aromatic, and of rather agreeable flavor. Quite coarse in appearance.

Savory or Summer Savory: An annual herb of the **Mint** family, with strong, agreeable, aromatic smell and flavor. Its leaves are in common use, both fresh and dried, for flavoring soups, etc. Dried Savory being retailed both loose and in cans and bottles.

The blossoms and branches are also sometimes similarly employed.

Thyme: A garden herb largely cultivated for its fragrant tops and leaves, which are popular as a culinary seasoning.

The best variety is the **Lemon Scented.**

Thyme for drying should be cut when just commencing to blossom, and should be slowly dried in the shade. It is sold in cans and bottles, or loose in small bunches.

Sage: A shrub whose tops and wrinkled, whitish-green leaves are extensively used, both fresh and dried, for flavoring soups, sauces, dressing, etc., because of its characteristic aromatic, bitter and slightly astringent flavor. Dried **Sage** is retailed in packages, cans and bottles.

Sage grows wild in many parts of **Southern Europe** and has long been under cultivation in all the temperate climates.

Hops: The Hop plant is a climber, found wild in **America, Europe** and **Asia.** It has been cultivated in **Germany** since the Ninth Century, and is now also an important crop in the United States, the chief producing sections being **New York** and the **Pacific Coast States.**

It is famous for the property of its blossoms in preserving beer from bacterial action, while also imparting to it an agreeably bitter taste, and it is medicinally valuable as a sedative and narcotic, whether taken internally or applied externally in the form of pillows, fomentation, etc.

The ancients ate the young **Hop** shoots as we do asparagus, and this custom is still prevalent in parts of **England** and **Germany.**

The roots of the vine are perennial, the top only dying in the winter. The vines, which twine with the sun, from right to left, are now generally trained on dropwires or strings, or on wire trellis work, the old style poles being employed in comparatively few sections.

The blossoms are harvested in the latter part of

August and the beginning of **September.** They are cured and kiln-dried and then baled.

In the choice of **Hops,** care should be taken to select those which are full of lupulin (the essential principal), free from mould, and bright and silky in appearance, that are the most powerfully odorous, and the most free from leaves, stems, scaly fragments and sticks, and which, when rubbed between the hands, impart, in the greatest degree, a yellowish tint, and a glutinous feeling to the skin. It is best also to select those which are tightly packed, as, unless they are very firmly pressed together and quite solid, they soon spoil in keeping.

Hoarhound, or **Horehound:** A bushy plant of the **Mint** family, native to the **South** of **Europe** and **Eastern** countries, growing about a foot high and with round, wrinkled, almost hairy ("hoary") leaves, which contain a bitter principle and volatile oil of aromatic, but not very agreeable, smell.

It is used as a flavor for candy and also in medicinal syrups, for its curative properties for coughs and other affections.

Garden Balm, Balm Mint, or **Lemon Balm:** An aromatic herb of the **Mint** family, with, generally, a marked **Lemon** odor. It is used chiefly for household culinary purposes and in the manufacture of liquors and perfumes.

Fennel, Common Garden or **Sweet Fennel:** Is a plant chiefly cultivated for its leaves, which are consumed both fresh, for garnishing, as a salad, etc., and cooked as a vegetable; in the latter case, generally tied in bunches and boiled with fish and certain other foods.

It is very popular in Italy, especially in the vicinity of **Naples.**

The seeds are also used for seasoning. Possiby a slight reminder of **Celery.**

MINTS, CRESS, LAVENDER AND OTHER HERBS, BERRIES, ETC.

Lavender: A perennial plant now grown principally for its flowers, which are used in making perfumes or for sale dried for "sachet bags," etc. It was formerly very popular as a "pot-herb," and is still used for flavoring jellies, etc.

Mint: A general name for a large number of perennial plants, the best known of which are the **Peppermint, Spearmint** and **Pennyroyal,** cultivated chiefly for the essential oil which contains their aromatic and medicinal principles.

About 90% of the supply of **Peppermint** and **Spearmint** oils is produced and distilled in an area which has **Kalamazoo, Michigan,** for its center and within a seventy-five mile radius from that city. Their chief uses are in medicine, confectionery, chewing-gum, liquors, etc.

Spearmint leaves are also used for mint sauce and other culinary purposes, and at one time popular for the flavoring of beverage, such as Mint **Julip.**

Pennyroyal was at one time extensively employed medicinally, but it is now grown only in comparatively small quantities, and is used almost exclusively for seasoning.

Dried Mint is retailed in packages, bottles and cans. It should always be kept in a dry place.

Catnip, or Catmint: A field plant growing wild throughout the **United States.** The leaves and young shoots, aromatic, pungent and more or less bitter, are used for seasoning and as a domestic remedy.

The leaves are best while the plant is blooming. They may be preserved by drying a few days, being afterward kept in a dry place.

Everyone is familiar with the pleasure a cat finds in playing with Catnip, and Catnip balls, containing a few pieces, are an article of regular sale.

Rosemary: A plant or shrub of the Mint family, native to the South of Europe and Asia Minor,, now widely cultivated. Its leaves, greyish in color and curled at the edges, are very fragrant and slightly stimulant. They are employed in seasoning and in manufacture of preserves, and are still used to a limited degree in liquors.

Parsley: A favorite kitchen herb, popular for garnishing and flavoring, for the latter purpose being sold both fresh and dried. Common Parsley is said to be native to Egypt, but is now thoroughly naturalized both here and in several European countries. The variety chiefly grown is the curley-leafed type. The finest received in the eastern markets comes from Bermuda.

In addition to its flavoring qualities, Parsley contains an essential oil which is mildly stimulating.

Tarragon: A small, aromatic herb used for flavoring vinegar, mustard, pickles, sauces, salads, etc.

It is sold green and dried, the latter both loose and in cans and bottles. A half pound of green Tarragon will flavor fifty-four gallons of Tarragon vinegar.

Hyssop: A small, bushy herb with leaves of aromatic and stimulant properties which grows wild in the South of Europe. The tops and flowers are used in making "Hyssop Tea."

Juniper Berries: The dark-blue, pungent, aromatic berries of the evergreen Juniper shrub, commercially important formerly because of their use in flavoring gin.

A nice flavor is given to corned beef by adding a muslin bagful of crushed Juniper Berries to the brine.

Hackberry or Sugarberry: The fruit of the Nettle Tree. It is of pleasing sweetness and aromatic flavor, and, like the American persimmon, is at its best after it has been touched by frost.

Cress or Pepper Grass: Applicable to a number

of pungent, flavored plants of the Mustard family, used as a condiment for garnishing and in salads. The leaves of the common variety are divided and frequently curled. Those of the broad-leaf type are slightly nochted on the edges.

It is generally sown with Mustard. Rape is frequently used instead of Mustard, however, many people preferring it, the flavor being less pungent, the leaves are stiffer and keep fresh longer.

Water-Cress: An aquatic plant of pungent, salty and rather bitter flavor, which is especially popular as a spring salad. It grows wild in many parts, flourishing best in running water, with sandy bottoms.

Water-Cress offers itself as a pleasant means of providing the body with a good supply of natural salts. It is more generally endowed with the natural salts in addition to potash and acids.

Angelica: An aromatic plant, native to the Alps, which grows wild in Europe, as far North as Iceland and Lapland.

The natives of the latter country use the fleshy roots as food and the stalks as medicine. Commercially, the young and tender leaf stalks and midribs are candied for sale as confectionery, and the roots and seeds have always been employed extensively to flavor gin.

Mugwort: A tall, perennial herb with woolly leaves, formerly popular, dried or fresh, as a seasoning and for flavoring beverages.

Chervil: A highly esteemed garden herb grown in all temperate climates, and very popular in the South. It is similar to Parsley, the curled being even handsomer.

Chervil Bilbur, or Turnip-Rooted Chervil, is a French variety grown for its roots, which resemble the Parsnip in shape and color. It is a very desirable vegetable, the flesh being sweet and delicate in flavor and almost floury in texture.

171

Laver: An edible seaweed found both on the **Atlantic** and **Pacific** Coasts. It is a food item of importance in **Asia,** and in some parts of **Europe.**

In **Scotland** and **Ireland,** under the name of "**Sloak**" or "**Slook,**" it is boiled and served with butter, pepper and vinegar, etc., or fried in bacon fat after boiling. It is especially good as an accompaniment for cold meats.

It is best to cook it in a porcelain sauce-pan, as it is liable to act on metals.

Laver is rich in protein, averaging from 30% to 35%.

Green Sloke: A green-spored seaweed of the same type as **Laver.**

Dulse: An edible seaweed growing on the coasts of **Scotland, Ireland** and **Japan.** It also grows abundantly on the **New England** and **Newfoundland** coasts. What is said to be the best **Dulse** known is gathered at considerable risk and hazard near **Hampton, Nova Scotia,** on the **Bay of Fundy,** found principally on the **South Shore** on all rocky reefs from **Digby Gut** to **Cape Blomidon.**

It is found at the extreme low-water mark, fastened securely to the rocks, and can only be gathered at a duration of about thirty or forty minutes, or during **extremely** low tide.

Many lives have been lost in the occupation of gathering **Dulse** on **Fundy Bay** by inexperienced pickers, gathering in the **Coves,** and on trying to return find themselves entirely cut off by water.

The plant is a **dark reddish brown,** tough and leathery, and is very slippery and slimey when gathered.

After gathering, it is washed thoroughly in salt water and hung up and brushed with a broom. and then layed on boards in the sun to cure. Great care should be used not to allow rain or fog to touch the crop while curing, and usually takes about ninety-six hours of sun to properly cure it.

It is impossible in the Nova Scotia climate to cure Dulse only in the Summer months.

The demand is much greater than the supply, and sells on the Boston market at from 50 cents to $1.00 per pound.

The leaves are from two to four inches wide, and often reach a length of twenty feet and more.

Dulse is eaten dry as a relish, cooked with butter to be eaten with fish, etc., or boiled in milk to be served as a vegetable.

Carragheen, Irish Moss, Pearl Moss: A species of edible seaweed named after the town of Carragheen, near Waterford, Ireland, found on the British Islands, the rocky shores of continental Europe and the Eastern Shores of the United States and Canada. Similar varieties abound also on other parts of the American coast.

The Carragheen of domestic use is obtained principally from New Hampshire and Massachusetts, the harvest season there extending from May to September.

After gathering, the plants undergo the same treatment and preparation given Dulse, being washed in salt water, brushed and cleaned and spread on the beach or boards to dry.

As marketed, Carragheen is in pieces three to four inches to a foot long, flexible and branching. Reddish-brown to pale yellow color, almost white.

Kelp or Bladder Weed: An edible seaweed distinguished by its streamer-like leaves, found on both Northern coasts. The largest variety, known as Giant Bladder Weed, has leaves which average thirty to forty feet in length, used in soups, for service with meals, etc., and boiled as a vegetable.

HORSERADISH, ALSO PLANTS OF THE ONION FAMILY

Wasabi: A Japanese plant whose root is grated for use like American **Horseradish**. It has an agreeably sharp taste, is being grown to a limited extent in the United States.

Horseradish: A plant allied to the **Nasturtium** or **Cress** family, naturalized in most temperate countries. It is grown for its white, fleshy, pungent roots, which are generally grated and mixed with vinegar for use as a relish or condiment with meats, oysters, etc.

When grated, should be kept in air-tight jars or bottles, as it loses its strength and pungency rapidly; always keep in a dark, cool place.

The roots may be left in the ground all Winter and dug as needed. After digging, they may be kept fresh for a considerable time by covering in cool sand or light soil.

Chives, or Cives: A plant of the **Onion** family, cultivated for its leaves, which grow in tufts resembling grass in appearance, but hollow like **Onion** leaves. It is a good substitute for **Onions**, especially in soups and stews.

Garlic: A vegetable similar to a small **Onion**, but with the bulb divided into ten or twelve sections known as "**Cloves.**" At certain seasons it abounds in many pastures, and imparts a very rank flavor to the milk and butter of cows which feed on it. Its main use in cookery is to flavor soups and sauces, and in salads, pickles, etc.

Leek: A form of **Onion** cultiavted for the blanched lower parts of the leaves, commonly called the "stem," and the bulbulous roots, both of which are used in cookery, chiefly in soups and stews. In flavor they resemble a very mild ordinary onion.

Cibol or Welsh Onion: A member of the Onion family, which is grown principally for its leaves; of mild onion flavor, used for seasoning, etc.

Shallot or Scallion: A spice vegetable of the **Onion** tribe, of stronger but more mellow flavor than the common **Onion;** used for flavoring, sauces, stews, etc.

The true **Shallot ranges in size** from a walnut to a small fig, is inclined to pear-shape, and has a thick outer skin shading from reddish to gray, the bulb underneath being greenish at the base and violet on the upper portion. It grows in **"Clove"** form, several cloves attached to a common disc.

New **Shallots** come on the market in June, but the dried is most popular and may be kept all year. The young leaves are used for seasoning.

COUMARIN

The Flavoring Principal of the Tonka Bean

Tonka, or Tonqua Bean: The dark, aromatic seed of the fruit of **Coumarouna-Odorato,** a **South American** tree.

The essential principal, known as **Coumarin,** is a white substance found in small white crystals, under the coat and between the lobes. Because of its similarity in aroma, **Tonka Beans,** or the extracted **Coumarin,** are frequently employed in the manufacture of imitation **Vanilla** Extract, and while they are heavier and somewhat coarser in flavor, and their commercial value not nearly so great as even the commoner **Vanilla Bean,** they, however, properly handled, make a most wonderful substitute or imitation, in fact, the average layman could not distinguish the true from the imitation.

They are also used extensively for perfuming and flavoring smoking and chewing tobacco.

They are also placed in wardrobes and trunks. They impart a pleasing odor and preserve cloths from moths.

Coumarin is also found in **Woodruff, Sweet Cloves** and several other plants, and is manufactured synthetically in considerable quantities.

Lemon Oil: For many years almost the entire supply of the Oil of the **Lemon rind** was produced in **Sicily,** and is still obtained largely by hand processes, the small factory output, which is darker in appearance, being principally employed to heighten the color of the hand-made oil.

The two most widely used methods are known as the "two-piece sponge" and the "three-piece sponge," the distinction referring to the number of pieces into which the rind is cut.

The former method generally produces oil with the smallest percentage of water to be afterwards separated, but that from the latter method is said to filter more rapidly and keep clean longer.

For the three-piece method, the lemons are cut

lengthwise into three slices (the pulp is first re-moved), the juice to be expressed and sold to the manufacturers of **Citric Acid,** and the residue to be used as animal food, and then the peel is put into large baskets and stored in a cool place for some hours until it is considered in the proper condition for pressing.

Each workman engaged in extracting the oil has in front of him a tin-lined copper bowl, and holds in his left hand a medium-sized sponge of superfine quality, which has previously been very carefully washed. He also holds other small sponges between the fingers of the same hand to prevent the loss of any of the oil, which is very volatile. With the right hand he takes a piece of the peel from the basket and squeezes it against the sponge, thus forcing the oil through the pores of the rind into the sponge. When the sponge is full of essence, it is squeezed into the bowl.

In order to make sure that the peel has yielded all the essence that can be pressed out by hand, the overseer from time to time tests the rejected peel by squeezing it close to a flame. If there is any essence left, it is forced through the flame and produces a flash of light. (Children often try the same experiment with orange peels.) The used peel is put into brine and sold to manufac-turers of "**Candied Lemon Peel.**"

When the bowls are full they are set aside for a short time, to permit the impurities to settle and then the contents are carefully decanted, the clear essence going into large tin-lined copper vessels. Before shipment, the product is passed through filter paper to purify it and give it lim-pidity, and is finally transferred to copper bottles of various standard sizes.

The quantity and quality of essence yielded varies according to the season. During November, December and January, when the greater part of the supply is manufactured, one thousand lemons will give about one and a halfpounds of essence.

Lemons not fully ripe are preferred, as they yield a larger quantity and a more fragrant quality than those fully matured. A small amount of essence is made during the spring and summer, but the product lacks the delicate fragrance of that made in the winter.

California, within the last few years, has developed into a great producer of high-grade **Lemon Oil** of excellent quality and considerable quantity. The methods employed are more modern than the foregoing. Machinery enters largely into the manufacture and has aided materially in giving us a good quality of **Lemon Oil** at a much lower price than we were formerly compelled to pay.

Vanillin or **Vanilline:** Unofficial Vanillas are those which, coming from the official plant, do not yet correspond with the official description, and also have some derived from other species.

To the former class belong the **Splits** and **Cuts** (often referred to in articles on the original) as well as several dark-skinned varieties, apparently from wild plants, called in the native **Cimmarona, Mestiza, Puerca, etc.**

To the latter class belong the **Pompona,** derived from **Pompona Scheide,** wild and uncultivated in the same region as the other, and believed by the natives to be the ancestor of **Planifolia,** they regarding the latter as a cultivation derived from one or more uncultivated species.

The pods of both are short, thick, rough and tough, and the odor rankly fruity, or pruney, in the latter respect quite resembling the **Tahiti** variety.

Vanillin has been reported in the flowers of several **Orchidaceoe.** It has also been reported in the fruits of one or more plants of the same family.

For commercial purposes, Vanillin is manufactured on a large scale, both in this country and abroad.

Ask the man you meet casually on the street tomorrow if 20% added to cost does not yield 20% profit. Ten to one, he will say "Yes." But it doesn't. Profit is rightly figured only on sales, says all commercial authorities.

To gain 20% you must add 25% to cost. The following schedule is worth copying and pasting up somewhere within easy sight and reach of the place where you work longest and hardest. It is absolutely accurate, and it will save you many a needless calculation:

Pct. Added to Cost.		Pct. Profit on Selling Price.
5	is	4¾
7½	is	7
10	is	9
12½	is	11⅛
15	is	13
16	is	14¼
17½	is	15
20	is	16 2/3
25	is	20
30	is	23
33 1/3	is	25
35	is	26
37½	is	27¼
40	is	28½
45	is	31
50	is	33 1/3
55	is	35½
60	is	37½
65	is	39½
66 2/3	is	40
70	is	41
75	is	42 2/3
80	is	44½
85	is	46
90	is	47½
100	is	50

TEA: The aristocratic household beverage for centuries.

COFFEE: The most democratic of drinks. It appeals alike to rich and poor—to men and women. No home so humble it cannot afford Coffee. No mansion so grand it can dispense with it. Everybody drinks **Coffee.**

SPICE: The world's appetizer for Ages.

Lightning Source UK Ltd.
Milton Keynes UK
UKOW06f1807140916

283002UK00025B/580/P